KIRTLAND'S WARBLER:
THE NATURAL HISTORY OF AN
ENDANGERED SPECIES

by

LAWRENCE H. WALKINSHAW

CRANBROOK INSTITUTE OF SCIENCE
BLOOMFIELD HILLS, MICHIGAN

Bulletin 58

© 1983 Cranbrook Institute of Science
Second Printing—1987

Library of Congress Catalog Card Number 83-72782

ISBN-87737-035-4
Printed in the United States of America

Edited by Christine E. Bartz, Mark Bergland,
and Mercedes S. Foster

This book is dedicated to the people who have tried, are trying, and will continue to try to save this endangered bird, with the hope that it will help them to save not only Kirtland's Warbler but other forms of wildlife as well.

PREFACE

The importance of studying endangered species is more evident now than ever before. Man's increasingly adverse impact on the environment is threatening the existence of more and more species of animals and plants. Careful studies of these species are vital to help us understand the reasons for their decline and to provide background necessary for efforts to preserve them.

Kirtland's Warbler is a prime example of an endangered species for which conservation efforts have been based on careful research covering several decades. In recent years, this warbler has been known to nest only in the northern third of the Lower Peninsula of Michigan and to winter only in the Bahamas. Counts of singing males have indicated that its population dropped from approximately 500 in 1961 to 201 in 1971. Since then, the population has remained near the latter level in spite of successful efforts to increase nesting success by removing thousands of cowbirds from the breeding grounds of the warbler. This suggests that the decline may have been stemmed, but the lack of increase of the warblers is grounds for serious concern. It is clear that we need to know much more about the biology of this rare and interesting bird, in spite of the excellent work already done on it.

Lawrence H. Walkinshaw is the latest of a series of distinguished ornithologists who have studied Kirtland's Warbler. The particular interests and abilities of each of these men are reflected in their publications on this bird. Norman A. Wood, whose name is associated with the discoveries of the breeding grounds and nest of the warbler, was a pioneer in the study of bird distribution in Michigan. Josselyn Van Tyne, a distinguished editor and authority on avian biology, contributed much to the understanding of the life history and migration of the species. Mayfield's book on the warbler, published before the population declined, is notable for the careful analysis of data and lucid writing; and, it provided the background needed for conservation efforts. Dr. Walkinshaw, a field ornithologist of enormous drive and ability, and a peerless collector of field data, has, among other things, monitored nesting success in the warbler and followed his interest in genealogy by tracing the family histories of many of his birds.

I hope that this monograph will convince any remaining skeptics of the value of careful research on endangered species and will provide a stimulus for continued work on Kirtland's Warbler and other endangered species.

Robert W. Storer
19 June 1979

TABLE OF CONTENTS

LIST OF TABLES

LIST OF FIGURES

CHAPTER 1

INTRODUCTION

Early History

Kirtland's Warbler (*Dendroica kirtlandii*), a member of the Wood Warblers (Parulidae) of eastern North America, is the largest and one of the rarest birds of its genus. It was first described by S. F. Baird (1852) from a male specimen taken by Charles Pease on 13 May 1851 near Cleveland, Ohio. Pease gave the bird to his father-in-law, Dr. Jared P. Kirtland, who in turn gave it to his friend Baird and to the Smithsonian Institution at Washington, D.C.

Van Tyne (1951: 540) described the discovery of the winter range:

> "The winter range of the Kirtland Warbler is almost as interesting and remarkable as its summer range, for the species is apparently the only North American bird which is restricted in winter to the Bahamas. . . . The location of the winter range was foreshadowed by Baird's discovery (1865: 207) of the October specimen taken at sea by Samuel Cabot in 1841, 'between Abaco and Cuba', but not until C. B. Cory's report (1879) of the specimen he collected on Andros (January 9, 1879) was the actual location of the winter range known. In 1884 both C. J. Maynard (by January 10) and Cory (by February 12) found the species on New Providence, collecting 24 and 4 specimens respectively. In 1886 the naturalists of the Fish Commission steamer *Albatross* added Watlings Island and Green Cay to the known winter range of the species." (Ridgway, 1891: 337, 338)

During the years 1879 to 1899, 71 specimens were taken on the Bahama Islands of Andros, Athol, Berry, Caicos, Cat, Eleuthera, Great Abaco, Green Cay, New Providence and Watlings Island and in 1902 a specimen was taken on Little Abaco (Mayfield 1960).

The first Michigan specimen, a female, was taken at Ann Arbor, Washtenaw County (Covert 1876). During the ensuing 27 years, six other specimens were taken in Michigan while even more were taken in Ohio. Three of the Michigan birds were taken in the Ann Arbor area. One was taken at

1

Battle Creek, one at Kalamazoo, and one was found dead at the Spectacle Reef Light House. To my knowledge only two sightings of Kirtland's Warblers in Michigan outside the breeding grounds have been confirmed since that time. One of these birds was collected and one was mist-netted during banding operations. These 19th century records, along with those from nearby states and the wintering area, led Van Tyne (1951) and Mayfield (1960, 1977) to believe that the species was most abundant during the 1880s and 1890s. During this period, the species may have had a much more extensive breeding range than in recent years. Possibly, intense parasitism by the Brown-headed Cowbird (*Molothrus ater*) was the cause of the decline in its numbers. Cowbirds apparently moved into Michigan from the west as forested regions were cleared. My own experience indicates that there were undoubtedly fewer cowbirds in the Battle Creek region before 1940. Michigan was settled later than its neighboring states and Ontario, thus cowbird pressure may have been relatively low in the jack pine (*Pinus banksiana*) plains of the northern portion of the Lower Peninsula. Yet, cowbirds were present and some cowbirds parasitism did occur during the years 1904–1910 (E. Arnold, in Mayfield 1962a). Barrows (1921), N. A. Wood (1926), and Leopold (1924) all considered the cowbird the worst enemy of Kirtland's Warbler.

Josselyn Van Tyne began studying Kirtland's Warbler in 1932 and continued to do so until his death in 1957. Aiding him in these studies were Andrew J. Berger, Betty and W. Powell Cottrille, William A. Dyer, Fred and Frances Hammerstrom, Harold F. Mayfield, Robert W. Storer, George M. Sutton, Milton Trautman, Dale Zimmerman, and the author. Results of this study were published in Mayfield's excellent book (1960). Singing males were counted in 1951 (Mayfield 1953), 1961 (Mayfield 1962a), and 1971 (Mayfield 1972a). Participants of the 1971 survey found only 201 singing males compared with 432 males in 1951 and 502 males in 1961, indicating a marked population decline.

Conservation Efforts

Since the Kirtland's Warbler singing counts showed the species was declining at an alarming rate and since forest fires had become less prevalent, the Michigan Department of Natural Resources set aside three tracts of 3,109 ha (4 sq. mi.) each in state forest land in three counties to be managed for the benefit of the species (Mayfield 1962a; Radtke and Byelich 1963). On two of these tracts, pines were planted in a special arrangement leaving numerous openings. All of these tracts have attracted nesting warblers (Byelich *et al.* 1976).

The U.S. Forest Service also began to study the problem and in 1961 established a management area of more than 1,600 ha (4,110 acres) in the

Huron National Forest in Oscoda County. Their goal was to maintain a portion of the tract in suitable condition for the nesting warbler. Kirtland's Warblers have nested in this area every year since its establishment. Plans are now under way to increase the acreage of suitable habitat.

The 1971 count of singing males revealed a severe decline in the number of breeding warblers and this led to the consideration of several emergency measures to save the species. A program to reduce parasitism by trapping and removing Brown-headed Cowbirds from principal nesting areas was begun in the spring of 1972 by the U.S. Fish and Wildlife Service, Division of Population Management, with assistance from the Michigan Department of Natural Resources, the U.S. Forest Service, the Michigan, Detroit and Pontiac Audubon Societies, and the Michigan Natural Areas Council. Research by Radabaugh and Cuthbert had revealed that cowbird control greatly increased the nesting success of Kirtland's Warblers, and the 1972 control program, advised by Cuthbert, was extremely successful.

This program has been expanded since 1973 so that cowbirds are controlled on virtually all nesting areas (Byelich *et al.* 1976). In 1972, 1973, and 1974, 2,200, 3,305, and 4,075 cowbirds, respectively, were removed from warbler habitat. Since 1974, a few more traps have been added to all major nesting regions and cowbirds have been removed with equal success. Cowbird removal begins during late April every year and continues until the middle of July. When warblers desert a given area, traps are moved to newly inhabited regions. To date, over 40,000 cowbirds have been removed from warbler habitats.

CHAPTER 2

MATERIALS AND METHODS

From 1966 through 1982, the number of days I spent in the field per season ranged from 2 to 55 for a total of 304 days. Field hours per season varied from 25 to 664, totaling 3,245 hours. From 1966 to 1971, field work was conducted only on the Artillery Range study area. In other years, field work was conducted in all study regions. Field work began at dawn and often continued until 2000–2100 hours. Warbler territories were located by finding singing males. When time permitted, the mate was also located. Sometimes the female was found almost immediately while at other times it took days to locate her. The male occasionally gave away the nest site by singing nearby. If he seemed disturbed when I approached and froze motionless a few meters from me, the nest always proved to be nearby. By far, the easiest method by which to locate the nest was to follow the female. Some males carried food to their incubating mates and often showed extreme determination to deliver the food in spite of my proximity. Other males never brought food to their mates. On occasion, when near a nest, I would flush the female out by gently tapping the vegetation with a stick near the point where she disappeared. This did not damage the vegetation, the nest, or the eggs. After the location of the nest was noted, it was rarely approached closer than three to four meters in order to minimize disturbance.

Adults were captured after the eggs hatched and the nestlings were several days old. Each individual was marked with a U.S. Fish and Wildlife Service aluminum band. In addition, each adult was uniquely marked with one colored band. These colored bands enabled individual birds to be recognized through binoculars. Ten colors or bicolors were used for a total of 66 possible combinations for each sex. Nestlings were banded on the right leg with one U.S. Fish and Wildlife Service aluminum band when they were six to nine days old (except in 1976 when they were banded on the left leg). No birds were captured or banded in 1975.

Adults were captured with mist nets. On rare occasions, a male was lured into a net by a tape recorded song. Adults, nestlings, and eggs (only deserted or unhatched eggs after 1972) were measured with calipers calibrated to 0.1 cm. Adult birds, nestlings, and eggs were weighed in the field with a studio scale accurate to 0.1 g. As soon as the bird was banded and its weight and measurements recorded, it was released. The majority were never captured again. During later years considerable effort was made to capture any bird seen wearing a single aluminum band because these birds almost always proved to be birds banded as nestlings (Table 1).

Study Areas:

Kirtland's Warblers were studied in 14 different nesting areas in the north-central portion of the Lower Peninsula of Michigan. The codes given for these regions in the following descriptions will be used throughout the text. *Artillery Range South* (ARS), Crawford County, T27N, R2W, sections 15, 16, and 17. This region burned on 19 August 1955 resulting in a 938 ha stand of jack pines interspersed with adequate clearings. The 1967 fire which created ARN reduced the size of this region to 610 ha.

Artillery Range North (ARN), Crawford County, T27N, R2W, sections 8 and 9 and a portion of the southeast corner of section 7. A fire in early May 1967 created about 567 ha of Kirtland's Warbler habitat consisting of jack pine mixed with jack-oak.

Lovells Management Area (LMA), Crawford County, T28N, R1W, including portions of sections 5 and 6. This region was planted in 1958 and 1960 with jack pines in rows 1.8 m apart with the trees in each row 1.2 m apart. Each planting consisted of 10 rows of trees alternated with the equivalent of 15 unplanted rows, resulting in dense growths of small trees interspersed with wide openings. Rows in these plantings were up to 1.2 km long and often followed the contour of the land. Plantings were bordered by natural growths of jack pine of a variety of heights. The planting in one region was bordered by a recently lumbered area. A total of 283 ha were planted in this area and a fire on the north side of the area in about 1958 created a small adjoining region. This entire area had only one singing male in 1982 (Douglas Middleton, verbal communication).

Pere Cheney Area (PC), Crawford County, T25N, R2W and R3W, including sections 1, 6, 7, and 12. This area of 197 ha burned on 12 May 1958.

Kyle Lake (KL), Crawford County, south of Kyle Lake, T27N, R2W, including sections 19 and 20. In 1968, 325 ha burned here as the result of artillery fire.

Fletcher Burn (F), Kalkaska County, T25N, R5W, including sections 23, 24, and 27. This region of 1,899 ha burned 8–13 May 1968.

Muskrat Lake (ML), Oscoda County, T27N, R1E, including section 13 located 2.4 km northeast of Red Oak. Three hundred eighty-one ha burned here on 17 April 1964.

Mack Lake (MaL), Oscoda County, T26N, R3E, southeast of Mio. Sev-

TABLE 1. Returns of Kirtland's Warblers Banded as Nestlings (by the Author) from Both First and Second Broods (1966–1977).

Year	Region	BFB	RFB	BSB	RSB	TB	TR
1966	ARS	2				2	
1967	ARS	2				2	
1969	ARS	4	1M			4	1M
1970	ARS	19	1M			19	1M
1971	ARS	10	1M			10	1M
1972	ARS	41	7M 1F	3		44	7M 1F
1972	LMA	16	4M 3F	11		27	4M 3F
1972	PC	5				5	
1973	ARS	31	1M 1F			31	1M 1F
1973	ARN	1				1	
1973	LMA	25	3M 3F	7	1F	32	3M 4F
1973	PC	9		9		18	
1974	ARS	36	2M			36	2M
1974	ARN	8		3		11	
1974	LMA	38	2M 4F	14		52	2M 4F
1974	ML	5				5	
1975	LMA	5	1F			5	1F
1976	ARN	15	2M			15	2M
1976	LMA	45	2F	13		58	2F
1976	ML	5				5	
1976	KL	7				7	
1977	ARN	11				11	
1977	LMA	18		4		22	
1977	ML	7				7	
1977	MaL			3		3	
1977	Og	7		2		9	
1977	R	5				5	
Totals		377	24M 15F	69	1F	446	24M 16F

BFB = Banded First Brood; RFB = Return First Brood; BSB = Banded Second Brood; RSB = Return Second Brood; TB = Total Banded; TR = Total Returns.

eral regions were burned here at different times. Some areas were also planted with jack pines and some with red pines.

Damon (Og), Ogemaw County, T24N, R1E, including sections 13, 18, and 24 near Damon. This area, approximately 1,416 ha in extent, burned in 1966 (J. Weinrich, personal communication).

St. Helen (R), Roscommon County, T23N, R1W, including section 11 near St. Helen. About 324 ha burned in this area in 1966.

North Down River Road (NDRR), Crawford County, T26N, R3W, section 1 south of North Down River Road. About 129 ha burned here in 1966 or 1967.

Canada Creek (CC), Montmorency County, T32N, R2E, including sections 15 and 22 and a small portion of Presque Isle County. Over 11,554 ha in this region burned 6–7 May 1939.

Red Oak (Os), Oscoda County, T27N, R1E, one area including section 22 (about 283 ha) and a nearby region including sections 11, 13, and 14 (485 ha) burned on 31 May 1925. The latter region burned again on 17 April 1964 creating the Muskrat Lake region in section 13.

Tawas (I), Iosco County, T22N, R7E, section 5. About 81 ha burned here in either 1945 or 1946.

I first studied Kirtland's Warblers in a region south of Lovells (T28N, R1W, section 33) during the years 1931 to 1945. This region consisted of about 300 ha which were burned in 1925. Another fire in either 1968 or 1969 burned about 259 ha in the same region (Pat Harwood, personal communication). This region was still in use in 1982. I made my first singing male count in 1931 in Crawford County (T28N, T1W, section 33), 4.8 km south of Lovells. There were 17 singing males in late May. I have made counts in many of the regions described above, particularly on the Artillery Range North and South. Many of these counts extended through the entire month of June. The results of these counts are summarized in Table 2.

Personal Field Work

R. E. Olsen, A. D. Tinker, and I first studied Kirtland's Warbler at Lovells, Crawford County, Michigan in 1931. I located 17 singing males and found my first nest at that time. Along with Humphrey Olsen and R. E. Olsen, I found a second nest on 16 June 1931. In 1932 I found two new nesting regions near Red Oak, Oscoda County. At this location I captured and banded a tame female warbler on 25 June 1932. This female was the first Kirtland's Warbler to wear a band. Josselyn Van Tyne banded a second Kirtland's Warbler one week later. I caught another female by hand in June 1938 and have caught several birds in this way since that time. In June 1940 I captured a male warbler with a minnow seine while he was feeding nestlings. This male was banded and released. I banded nine nestlings in 1938, five nestlings in 1940, four nestlings in 1944, three nestlings and one adult female in 1948, and a pair of adults (captured with a minnow seine) in 1957.

I used a mist net for the first time in the Kirtland's Warbler habitat during 1966. From 1966 through 1977, I banded 61 adult females, 59 adult males, and 446 nestlings which fledged. Thirty-one banded nestlings were taken by predators and thus did not fledge. I also captured two adult males and one adult female banded by Frank Novy, two adult males banded by E. J. Slomkowski, three females and one male banded by Bruce Radabaugh, and one female and two males banded by Craig Orr. Warren Faust and I captured and banded a male who was feeding fledglings at Boon, Wexford County,

TABLE 2. Singing Male Kirtland's Warblers Counted by the Author.

Area	1966	1967	1968	1969	1970	1971	1972	1973	1974	1975	1976	1977	1978	1979	1980	1981	1982
LMA						12	19	30	24	31	32	28	23	12	9	2	1
ARS	59*	0		68*		62	53	49	26	25	7	4	0	0	0	0	0
ARN			0	0	0	0	1	8	19	28	34	33	31	35#	49#	39#	—
PC	19					23	24	26	21	9	9	7	5	8	11	3	1
ML							4	12	14	16	15	25	21	31	29	27	—

*approximate singing male population
#counts recorded by Ryel (1979a, 1980, 1981).
The figures for 1979, 1980 and 1981 are official counts; other numbers reflect total male populations.

Michigan on 2 July 1972. With Paul Aird, we captured and banded an adult male at Petawawa, Ontario on 1 July 1977. In summary, I have banded 626 individuals and have captured 12 birds banded by others for a total of 638 Kirtland's Warblers (Tables 3 and 4).

The regions in which Kirtland's Warbler nestlings were banded during the 1966 to 1977 breeding seasons are detailed in Table 1. Of the 446 nestlings banded, 412 were banded in Crawford County. This includes 196 from the Lovells Management Area, 38 from the Artillery Range North, 148 from the Artillery Range South, 23 from Pere Cheney, and 7 from Kyle Lake. Twenty nestlings were banded in Oscoda County including 17 from Muskrat Lake and 3 from Mack Lake. Five nestlings were banded near St. Helen, Roscommon County, and nine nestlings were banded near Damon, Ogemaw County.

In 1933 Alfred Dowding and I searched both northern Wisconsin and the

TABLE 3.   Banded Adult Male Kirtland's Warblers Present Each Year on Study Areas.

Year	AMB	PBAM	MR	MR(ASY)	TMWB
1964	1	—	—	—	1
1965	2	1	0	0	3
1966	5	3	0	0	8
1967	4	6	0	0	10
1968	0	8	0	0	8
1969	4	8	0	0	12
1970	9	7	1	0	17
1971	6	8	1	1	16
1972	8	10	2	2	22
1973	4	7	11	4	26
1974	9	5	4	12	30
1975	0	9	6	14	29
1976	9	7	0	16	32
1977	2	11	2	12	27
1978	0	10	0	8	18
1979	0	4	0	5	9
1980	0	2	0	2	4
1981	0	2	0	2	4
1982	0	1			1
TOTALS	63	109	27	78	277

AMB, adult males banded during that year; PBAM, previously banded adult males which returned during that year; MR, males banded as nestlings which returned when one year old; MR(ASY), males banded as nestlings which returned when two or more years of age; TMWB, total number of adult males known alive that year. Figures for 1964–1971 include Artillery Range Study Area only.

TABLE 4.   Banded Adult Female Kirtland's Warblers Present Each Year
on Study Areas.

Year	AFB	PBAF	FR	FR(ASY)	TFWB
1966	3	—	—	—	3
1967	5	0	0	0	5
1968	1*	0	1**	0	2
1969	5	1	1**	1	8
1970	9	3	0	2	14
1971	5	5	1**	1	12
1972	11	7	0	2	20
1973	6	9	4	2	21
1974	5	6	5	5	21
1975	0	4	5	6	15
1976	8	3	1	6	18
1977	4	5	2	4	15
1978	0	3	0	1	4
1979	0	0	0	0	0
1980	0	0	0	0	0
Totals	62	46	20	30	158

AFB, adult females banded during that year; PBAF, previously banded adult females
which returned during that year; FR, females banded as nestlings which returned
when one year old; FR(ASY), females banded as nestlings which returned when two
or more years old; TFWB, total number of females wearing bands. *, one adult
female in 1968 was banded by Frank Novy; **, three separate females banded by
Bruce Radabaugh at Mack Lake, Oscoda Co., nested on my study areas, 1968, 1969
and 1971 (ARS, 2; ML, 1). Figures for 1966–1971 include Artillery Range Study
Area only.

Upper Peninsula of Michigan in an attempt to locate other warbler nesting
areas. Since that time I have studied this species in Presque Isle County,
Montmorency County, Kalkaska County, Crawford County, Oscoda County,
Wexford County, Roscommon County, Ogemaw County, and Iosco County
locating nests or fledged nestlings in each of these counties. I have also
searched several other counties in the Lower Peninsula both west and southwest of the known breeding regions.

During late June and early July of 1966, Harriet and Kenneth Krum, William Coates, William A. Dyer, and I visited a new Kirtland's Warbler colony 19–23 km northeast of Grayling, Crawford County hoping to take mov-
ies and still photographs. Out of eight nests observed in this region only
two nestling Kirtland's Warblers were fledged. The other nests fledged only
cowbirds. As a result, for several years following this discovery, William
A. Dyer and I studied this species each June and July and removed cowbird

eggs and nestlings from parasitized warbler nests. From 1972 to 1977 I was assisted in my field studies by Warren Faust, a graduate student from the University of Michigan working on Kirtland's Warbler vocalizations. During the 1967 and 1968 breeding seasons, I was assisted in the field by my grandsons, Ronald and Steven Walkinshaw.

CHAPTER 3

PHYSICAL CHARACTERISTICS OF KIRTLAND'S WARBLER

Adult Plumages

Kirtland's Warbler (*Dendroica kirtlandii*) is one of the larger wood warblers (Parulidae). It is the largest of its genus and is similar to the Connecticut Warbler in size. It acquires its spring plumage between February and April (Mayfield 1960). In spring plumage, the adult male is a beautiful blue-gray on the head, back, and less so on the tail where many of the feathers are streaked along the long shafts with black. There are two distinct wing bars. The male has black lores and both eyelids are white, forming an almost complete eye ring. The breast and sides of the breast are bright yellow with black streaks along the sides. The legs and feet are black or nearly so. First-year males have additional fine streaks across the upper breast as well as along the sides. At times, their black lores are poorly defined.

The adult female is much duller in color than the male having a more brownish-gray tinge above, a duller yellow below, and finer streakings on the sides of the breast and on the upper breast. She lacks the black lores which are present in the adult male. Both males and females have small white spots on the outer two tail feathers near the tips and rarely a very small white area on the third. First-year females are almost identical to older birds, but may have more fine black streakings below.

Kirtland's Warbler molts again during late July and August. The male now more closely resembles the female. His coloring is much more brownish on the head and back and the black lores are either absent or very faint. During their first molt, juvenal Kirtland's Warblers and juvenal Palm Warblers are very similar in appearance and both wag their tails. This post juvenal molt in Kirtland's Warbler begins at about 26 days and is completed at 43 days (Mayfield 1960). The time frame is probably about the same for the Palm Warbler. When the final adult plumage is acquired these species do not resemble each other.

Similar Warbler Species

Kirtland's Warbler has a distinctive habit of bobbing its tail up and down. Most of the species with which it might be confused do not do this. It inhabits jack pine forests of largely uniform height during the summer and low brushy shores in the Bahamas during the winter. During migration it may be found in areas where other warbler species are found.

Those species which may be mistaken for Kirtland's Warbler are the Magnolia Warbler, the Yellow-throated Warbler, and the Yellow-rumped Warbler. The Magnolia Warbler inhabits hemlock and spruce forests in summer; it is a smaller bird than Kirtland's Warbler. It always has a black band on the tip of the tail and it also has white spots on the five outer tail feathers. It has a yellow breast and a yellow rump. The Yellow-throated Warbler is a more southern bird than Kirtland's Warbler. It has black lores and a yellow throat, but it has a white belly and does not wag its tail as Kirtland's Warbler does. The Yellow-rumped or Myrtle Warbler has much black below, a white breast, and a yellow rump. The female is not as heavily marked as the male but she always has a yellow rump. Both males and females have white spots on three outer tail feathers.

Weights and Measurements of Adults

Mayfield (1960) reported a sample of 64 adult male Kirtland's Warblers which had an average weight of 13.7 ± 0.6 g and 13 adult females with an average weight of 14.2 ± 1.1 g. Nineteen males that I weighed in the field varied between 12.4 g and 15.3 g for an average weight of 13.7 ± 1.1 g. Sixty-two male museum specimens from the University of Michigan Museum of Zoology had recorded weights of 12.5 g to 15.8 g ($\bar{x}$ = 13.8 g). The combined weights of these 81 adult males yielded an average weight of 13.7 ± 0.8 g. All of these males were at least one year old. I also weighed 18 adult females in the field. These individuals combined with 14 recorded specimens from the University of Michigan Museum of Zoology had an average weight of 13.8 ± 1.1 g (range, 12.2 g to 16.0 g).

Wing chord measurements of 69 adult male Kirtland's Warblers taken in the field varied between 64.0 mm and 75.0 mm. The average length was 70.1 ± 2.5 mm. Wing chord measurements of 124 male museum specimens (UMMZ) ranged between 66.0 mm and 75.0 mm. The average value for these specimens was 70.5 ± 1.9 mm. Tail measurements were recorded for 139 males, both field and museum specimens. Four of these tails were rather short with some sheaths still present at their bases (45.0 mm, 47.2 mm, 48.2 mm, 49.0 mm). The maximum tail measurement was 64 mm while the average length for all 139 males was 57.0 ± 3.1 mm.

TABLE 5.   Weights, Wing Chord, Tail, and Tarsal Measurements of
Adult Kirtland's Warblers.

	N	Males	N	Females
Weight in g				
Adults in field	19	13.7 ± 1.1		
Specimens (UMMZ)	62	13.8 ± 0.6		
Above combined	81	13.7 ± 0.8	32	13.8 ± 1.1
Extremes		12.4–15.8		12.2–16.0
Wing Chord in mm				
Adults in field	69	70.1 ± 2.5	71	65.6 ± 2.0
Specimens (UMMZ)	124	70.5 ± 1.9	50	66.7 ± 2.5
Extremes		64.0–75.0		60.3–73.8
Tail in mm				
Both field and				
specimens	139	57.0 ± 3.1	103	55.6 ± 2.6
Extremes		45.0–64.0		50.0–63.0
Tarsus in mm	43	21.7 ± 1.0	45	21.1 ± 1.0
Extremes		19.0–23.5		19.0–22.5
Expanse in mm	4	212.0	1	208.0
Extremes		210.0–214.0		
Length in mm	4	152.0	2	150.0
Extremes		151.0–153.0		149.0–150.0

One-year-old males had shorter wings than older adult males. Wing chords of seven year-old males had an average length of 67.5 mm (range, 65.7 mm to 69.0 mm). Their tail measurements varied between 53.3 mm and 59.0 mm ($\bar{x}$ = 56.3 mm). Four males known to be two years old had wing measurements that varied between 67.0 mm and 72.2 mm ($\bar{x}$ = 69.2 mm) and tail measurements that varied between 54.8 mm and 59.0 mm ($\bar{x}$ = 57.3 mm). Compared to other *Dendroica*, Kirtland's Warbler has a very long tarsus which is quite noticeable when the bird is standing on a branch. Tarsal lengths of 43 males varied between 19 mm and 23.5 mm ($\bar{x}$ = 21.7 ± 1.0 mm).

Wing chord measurements of 71 female Kirtland's Warblers at least one year old were taken in the field. These measurements varied between 60.3 mm and 69.4 mm ($\bar{x}$ = 65.6 ± 2.0 mm). Fifty museum specimens (UMMZ) had wing chords that varied between 62.5 mm and 73.8 mm ($\bar{x}$ = 66.7 ± 2.5 mm). Tail measurements of 69 adult females were also taken in the field. These tail lengths varied between 50.0 mm and 63.0 mm ($\bar{x}$ = 55.6 ± 2.6 mm). Tail measurements of 34 female museum specimens (UMMZ) ranged between 51.4 mm and 60.0 mm ($\bar{x}$ = 54.9 ± 2.2 mm). Tarsal measurements of 45 females, both field and museum specimens, ranged between 19.0 mm and 22.5 mm ($\bar{x}$ = 21.1 ± 1.0 mm).

Eight females known to be one year old had wing chords measuring between 60.3 mm and 67.2 mm ($\bar{x}$ = 64.7 mm) and tails measuring between 53 mm and 58.3 mm ($\bar{x}$ = 56.3 mm). Three females known to be two years old had wing chord measurements of 61.8 mm, 66.3 mm, and 67.7 mm and tail measurements of 48.7 mm, 54.8 mm, and 56.9 mm. One of these females had a tarsal measurement of 22.5 mm.

CHAPTER 4

DISTRIBUTION

Winter

Van Tyne (1951) has detailed the winter distribution of Kirtland's Warbler. The only place the species has ever been found in winter is the Bahama Islands. The sight records, with the exception of two, were substantiated by specimens. The following are the islands where the species has been sighted in winter (with the number of sightings indicated): Andros, 1; Berry, 3; Caicos, 2; Cat, 1; Cat Cay, 1; Eleuthera, 10; Great Abaco, 1; Great Inagua, 1; Green Cay, 2; Little Abaco, 1; New Providence, 46; Watlings Island, 4. The first report of the species in winter was made by C. B. Cory (1879) when he collected one on Andros Island on 9 January 1879. Van Tyne (1951: 540) further detailed the winter range of the species:

> "In 1884 both C. J. Maynard (by January 10) and Cory (by February 12) found the species on New Providence, collecting 24 and 4 specimens respectively. In 1886 the naturalists of the Fish Commission Steamer, *Albatross*, added Watlings Island and Green Cay . . . The following year, A. H. Jennings . . . collected 8 specimens on New Providence during some general field work which began March 12, though Maynard . . . failed to find the bird there during November and December. J. Percy Moore collected a specimen at Port Howe, Cat Island, on November 20, 1890 (Academy of Natural Sciences of Philadelphia collection). In 1891 C. S. Winch added Eleuthera, and Maynard collected additional specimens there in 1897. Cory . . . and his collector Winch found the species on the Berry Islands and on Caicos (the latter still the southeasternmost record for the species) in 1891. Small collections made by Maynard in 1893 and 1897 on New Providence complete the nineteenth century records . . . In 1902 J. L. Bonhote added a record for Little Abaco and took one . . . on New Providence."

Cory (1879) took a specimen at Hawks Nest, Andros Island on 9 January 1879. In 1886 he added New Providence Island to the range and in 1892 he added Berry Island, Eleuthera, Grand Caicos and East Caicos. Ridgway (1891) took four specimens on Watlings Island 4–9 March (1891?) and two specimens on Green Cay. Maynard (1881 and 1896) listed 26 records for Nassau, New Providence and one record for Southern Bight, Andros Island. Bangs (1900) reported two specimens taken at Nassau on 4 March 1897 and 5 April 1897. Bonhote (1903) reported that he took a male on 25 March 1902 on Little Abaco. Chapman (1908) reported sighting the bird on 27–28 April 1907 on Cat Cay. Bond (1951) took a specimen at Port Howe, Cat Island on 20 November (1950?). Challinor (1962) saw a male on 27 March 1957 on Hog Island, while Blanchard (1965) sighted one on 16 November 1963 at Grand Bahama. Wallace (1968) saw one on 27 August 1967 near Nassau, while Robertson (1971) sighted one at Nassau on 20 August 1970. Radabaugh (1974) observed a male on 11, 12, and 22 March 1973 on Crooked Island and Clench (1978) sighted a female warbler on 10 February 1978 at North Caicos.

Spring Migration

After leaving the Bahama Islands, Kirtland's Warblers migrate in a northwestern direction generally arriving in Florida, Georgia, and South Carolina by the latter part of April. They arrive in Ohio by early May and many males are found on the Michigan breeding grounds by 10–11 May. The following are spring records of captured, photographed, or sighted birds:

Florida:

Martin County: W. Jupiter, 27 April 1897 (spec.) by C. B. Cory (1898); W. Jupiter, 19 April 1897 (sighting) by C. B. Cory (1898).
Alachua County: Gainesville, 26 April 1934 (sighting) by R. C. McClanahan (1935).

Georgia:

Camden County: Cumberland Island, 12 April 1902 (♀ spec.) by A. H. Helme (1904); Cumberland Island, 14 April 1903 (♀ spec.) (Greene, *et al.* 1945); Cumberland Island, 27 April 1904 (♂ spec.) (Greene, et al. 1945); 16 April 1902 (spec.) (Greene, *et al.* 1945).

Alabama:

Coosa County: Woodbine, 10 May 1908 (♂ sighting) by A. A. Saunders (1908).

South Carolina:

Beaufort County: St. Helena Island, 27 April 1886 (♂ spec.) by W. Hoxie (1886).

Cherokee County: Gaffney, 5 May 1925 (sighting, one ♂ and one ♀) by P. M. Jenness (1925).

Ohio:

Champaign County: Urbana, 14 May 1909 (♂ sighting) (Petry 1909).
Cuyahoga County: Rockport, 13 May 1851 (♂ spec.) by C. Pease (Baird 1852); Rockport, May 1878 (♂ and ♀ specs.) by W. and J. Hall (Wheaton 1879); Cleveland, 4 May 1880 (♂ spec.) and 12 May 1880 (♀ spec.) (Langdon 1880).
Franklin County: Indian Springs, May 1917 (sighting) (Thomas 1926); Columbus, 20 May 1920, 17 May 1921, 23 May 1924, 24 May 1924 (sightings) (Thomas 1926); Columbus, 21–23 May 1917 (sighting) (Jones 1917).
Hamilton County: Cincinnati, early May 1872 (♂ spec.) by C. Dury (Purdie 1879).
Lorain County: Oberlin, 9 May 1900 (one captured) by L. Jones (1910); Oberlin, 7 May 1900, 9 May 1900, 2 May 1906 (sightings) by L. Jones (1900, 1902, 1906).
Ottawa County: Catawba Point, 15 May 1909 (♂ spec.) (Henninger 1912). Magee Marsh Wildlife Refuge, 21 May 1980 female specimen captured, banded, photographed, and released by E. Tramer (Kleen 1980).
Preble County: New Paris, 13 May 1905 (sighting) (Petry 1909).
Seneca County: 11 May 1906 (two sightings) by W. F. Henninger (1906); New Bremen, 14 May 1908 (sighting) by W. F. Henninger (1908).
South Bass Island: Put-in-Bay, 24 May 1954 (♀ spec.) by M. Trautman (Mayfield 1960).

Indiana:

Hamilton County: 14 May 1950 (sighting) (Marks and Wright 1950).
Porter County: Chesterton, 17 May 1981, a female was photographed by K. J. Brock (1982).
Randolph County: 21 May 1950 (sighting) (Marks and Wright 1950).
Wabash County: Wabash, 4 May 1892 (spec.) and 7 May 1895 (♂ spec. UMMZ) by W. O. Wallace (Ulrey and Wallace 1895).
Wayne County: Richmond, 13 May 1905 (♀ spec.) by L. C. Petry (Dennis 1905); Richmond, 7 May 1906 (sighting) and 18 May 1908 (♀ sighting) by M. S. Markle (Petry 1909).

Illinois:

Cook County: Chicago, Morgan Park, 22 May 1899 (♂ spec.) by E. Blackwelder (1899); Chicago, 21 May 1899 (sighting) (Smith and Parmalee 1955).
DuPage County: Glen Ellyn, 7 May 1894 (♂ spec.) by B. T. Gault (1894).

Tazewell County: Tremont, 25 May 1918 (sighting) and 9 May 1924 (sighting) (Ford, et al. 1934).
Winnebago County: 25 May 1894 (spec.) (Cory, 1909); 25 May 1894 (sighting) (Smith and Parmalee 1955).
"Bird Haven," 3 May 1908 (♂ sighting) by R. Ridgway (1914).

Missouri:

St. Louis County: St. Louis, 8 May 1885 (♂ spec.) by O. Widmann (1885).

Minnesota:

Hennepin County: Minneapolis, 13 May 1892 (♂ Spec. MMNH) by H. M. Guilford (1893).

Massachusetts:

Suffolk County: Roslindale, 26 May 1916 (sighting) by J. W. Sherman (Forbush 1929).

West Virginia:

Monongalia County: Morgantown, 9 May 1937 (sighting) and 16 May 1943 (sighting) by I. B. Boggs (1944); Coopers Rock State Park, 19 May 1937 (sighting) by M. Brooks and I. B. Boggs (1937).

Wisconsin:

Racine County: Racine, 20 May 1853 (sic) (sighting) by P. R. Hoy (1852).
Jefferson County: near Lake Koshkonong, 24 May 1893 bird shot, captured, and escaped by L. Kumlien and N. Hollister (1903).
Dane County: Madison, 19 May 1917 (sighting) (Taylor 1917).
Outagamie County: Appleton, 19 May 1941 (sighting) by W. Rogers (Barger 1941).
Oneida County: Rhinelander, 23 May 1946 (sighting) (Kumlien and Hollister 1951).
Door County: 40 km northeast of Green Bay, 20 May 1956 (sighting) by R. and C. Hussong (1956).
Brown County: Green Bay, 25–26 May 1967 (sighting) by B. Columban (1968).
Washara County: Redgranite, 21 May 1971 (sighting) by D. Greenman (1972).
Jackson County: Black River Falls, 7 June 1979 (♂ sighting) by D. Follen (1980); Black River Falls, 10 June 1978 (two ♂ sightings) (Tessen 1978); 14 June 1980 (♂ sighting) (Tessen 1980).

Michigan:

Calhoun County: Battle Creek, 11 May 1883 (δ spec. USNM) by N. Y. Green (Ridgway 1884).
Mackinac County: Spectacle Reef Lighthouse, 21 May 1885 (δ spec. UMMZ) by W. Marshall (Merriam 1885).
Kalamazoo County: Kalamazoo, 15 May 1886 ($\female$ spec. UMMZ) by F. H. Chapin (Gibbs 1898; Van Tyne 1939).
Washtenaw County: Scio, 15 May 1875 ($\female$ spec. UMMZ) and 16 May 1879 ($\female$ spec. UMMZ) by A. B. Covert (1876, 1881); Ann Arbor, 18 May 1888 (δ spec. UMMZ) by L. Knapp (Washburn 1889); Ann Arbor, 14 May 1902 ($\female$ spec. UMMZ), 6 May 1905 (δ sighting), 13–16 May 1907 (sighting), 10 May 1911 (sighting) (Wood 1902, 1903, 1905, 1908, 1912).
Tuscola County: Fish Point, 21 May 1926 ($\female$ spec. UMMZ) by N. A. Wood (1951).
Oscoda County: Six miles south of Mio, 13 May 1956 (two δ spec. UMMZ) by J. Van Tyne.
Monroe County: Erie Game Area, 10 May 1969 (one pair sighted) (Kelley 1969).
Wayne County: Hamtramck, 30 May 1907 (sighting) by J. C. Wood (1908).
Saginaw County: 10 May 1955 (sighting) (Black 1955).
Ottawa County: Holland, 22 May 1938 (sighting) and 10–11 May 1963 (two sightings) by A. B. Schroeder and T. B. DeBlaey (1968).

Canada:

Ontario:
Essex County: Point Pelee National Park, 10 May 1953 (sighting), 10 May 1959 (sighting) and 13 May 1961 (sighting) by G. M. Stirrett (1973); Point Pelee National Park, 10 May 1959 male banded and released by J. Woodford (1959); Point Pelee National Park, 13 May 1961 bird photographed (Aird and Hibbard 1978).
York County: Toronto, 16 May 1900 (δ spec. ROM) by J. H. Samuel (1900); Toronto, 16–20 May 1958 (sighting) and 24 May 1959 (sighting) by Baillie (Aird and Hibbard 1978); Toronto, 30 May 1947 (sighting) (Aird and Hibbard 1978).
Prince Edward County: Point Traverse, 19 May 1962 (sighting) (Sprague 1969); Cataraqui Cemetery, 12 May 1964 (sighting) (Sprague 1969).
Renfrew County: Petawawa Military Camp, 2 June 1978, a banded male returned (Chamberlain and McKeating 1978).
Simcoe County: Barrie, 16–20 May 1964 a male photographed and remained for several days (Aird and Hibbard 1978); Barrie, 19 May 1967 (Devitt 1967).

Ontario County: Whitby, 19 May 1962, 1 June 1963 and 14–19 May 1979 (Goodwin 1963, 1979).

Quebec:
Gatineau Valley, Kazabazua (lat. 45°57', long. 76°02'), 27 May 1978, a banded male captured (Chamberlain and McKeating 1978).

Many records are available documenting the arrival of Kirtland's Warbler on its nesting grounds. The majority of these are from the period since 1972. Since that time, U.S. Fish and Wildlife Service personnel have been working on the jack pine habitat daily from late April until August. In many cases, they have recorded the arrival of the first males. The following observations of male arrivals on the nesting grounds show remarkable uniformity:

Crawford County: 10 km west of Grayling, 13 May 1937 (1) (Walkinshaw), 22 May 1959 (1) (Kenaga 1959), 22 May 1960 (Kenaga 1960), 11 May 1963 (2) (Cuthbert 1964); Artillery Range North and South, 12 May 1972, 14 May 1973, 12 May 1974, 14 May 1975, 12 May 1976, 11 May 1977, 14 May 1978, and 11 May 1981; North Down River Road, 10 May 1982; Lovells Management Area, 13–14 May 1977 (12) (Walkinshaw) and 12 May 1978 (D. Middleton, personal communication); Pere Cheney, 12 May 1976 (U.S. Forest Service).

Oscoda County: Mack Lake, 6 miles southeast of Mio, 13 May 1972, 14 May 1973, 12 May 1976, 11 May 1977, and 14 May 1978; Mio, 10 May 1953 (Wickstrom 1953), 9 May 1964 (15) (Wallace 1965).

Ogemaw County: Damon, 17 May 1973, 12 May 1977, 16 May 1978, 14 May 1980 (10+), and 12 May 1981 (1) (J. Weinrich, personal communication).

Kalkaska County: Fletcher Burn, 8 May 1949 (2), 14 May 1954, 12 May 1955 (Black 1949, 1954, 1955).

Montmorency County: Clear Lake, 21 May 1960 (12) (Kenaga 1960).

Iosco County: 5 miles northwest of Tawas City, 21 May 1952 (3♂) (Wickstrom 1952a, 1952b).

Summer Range

Breeding regions of Kirtland's Warbler have been found only in Michigan between 44° and 45° 20' north latitude and between 83°35' and 86° west longitude, a somewhat triangular-shaped area approximately 138 km from north to south and 177 km from east to west. Not all of this region is forested with jack pines and much of the existing jack pine habitat is not used by Kirtland's Warbler (Figures 1 and 2). Kirtland's Warbler has been found in summer in the following Michigan counties: Alcona, Alpena, Clare, Crawford, Iosco, Kalkaska, Montmorency, Presque Isle, Ogemaw, Oscoda, Otsego, Roscommon and Wexford. I have observed the species in all of these counties except Alcona, Alpena, Clare, and Otsego, none of which has ever had a large population. I have seen a total of 341 nests distributed in the following counties: 290 nests in Crawford County, 27 nests in Oscoda County, 19 nests in Ogemaw County, and 1 nest each in Iosco, Montmorency, Presque Isle, and Roscommon Counties. I have also seen fledglings in Wexford County. During 1982, John Probst found a singing male near Gwinn in Marquette County (personal communication). Over the past ten years the species has become more restricted in the Lower Peninsula so that it now occupies only the following six counties: Kalkaska, Crawford, Oscoda, Roscommon, Ogemaw, and Iosco. Since record keeping began, the majority of Kirtland's Warblers have been found in Crawford County and Oscoda County.

Vim A. van Eck (in litt.) found several singing males at a plantation in Newaygo County, 8 km southeast of White Cloud, in 1954 and 1955. This region is 85 km south of Boon, Wexford County, which is the most western documented breeding region. I visited Newaygo County in 1978 and found a mature growth of jack pines on very sandy soil much like the habitat in Oscoda and Crawford Counties. In Presque Isle County, the northernmost documented breeding region, Pettingill (1958) recorded two to five singing males during the years 1951 to 1957. There are several records of singing males outside the documented breeding range, suggesting that the species is able to breed at or near the same latitude if conditions are favorable. Harrington (1939) reported that male Kirtland's Warblers were not uncommon at the Petawawa Military Camp near Pembroke, Ontario in 1916. He revisited the region in 1939 and found one singing male. Paul Aird (Aird and Hibbard 1978) found a lone singing male at Petawawa Military Camp on 8 June 1977. It remained on the territory well into July. This bird was captured, banded, photographed, and released on 1 July 1977. It returned to Petawawa in 1978. Another singing male was found in Ontario on the Bruce Peninsula near McVicar on 8–30 June 1958 (Gunn 1958). Paul Aird and his Canadian team captured by mist net another banded male in the Gatineau River valley, north of Ottawa in the province of Quebec (Chamberlain and McKeating 1978). This bird remained in the area through the month of June; it had been banded as a nestling in Michigan.

Nancy Tilghman (1979) discovered two singing males near Black River Falls, Jackson County, Wisconsin, during the 1978 breeding season. On 21 June 1978, John Byelich, Nancy Tilghman and I captured one of these males. It was wearing a band I had placed on it when it was a nestling on the ARS, Crawford County, Michigan, on 29 June 1972. At least one of these males returned to the Black River Falls area in 1979 (Follen 1980). It should be

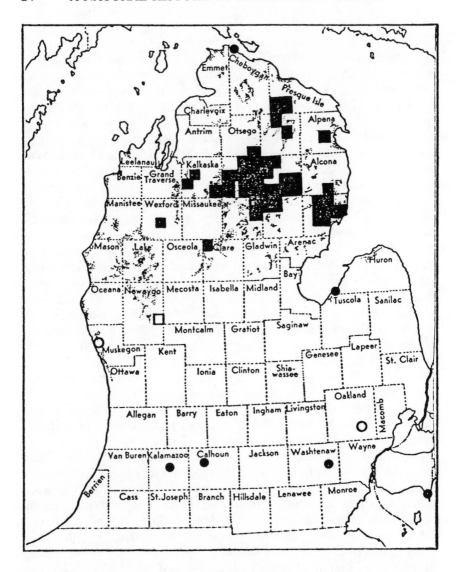

FIGURE 1.   Known Nesting Regions of Kirtland's Warbler in Michigan
from 1903 through 1982. This is an updated version of the map presented
by Mayfield (1960). Stippling indicates natural stands of jack pine from
Zimmerman (1956).
Black circles = spring sightings
Open circles = fall sightings
Open square = possible breeding season sighting (see text for details)
Black rectangles = 6 mi or 9.7 km per square

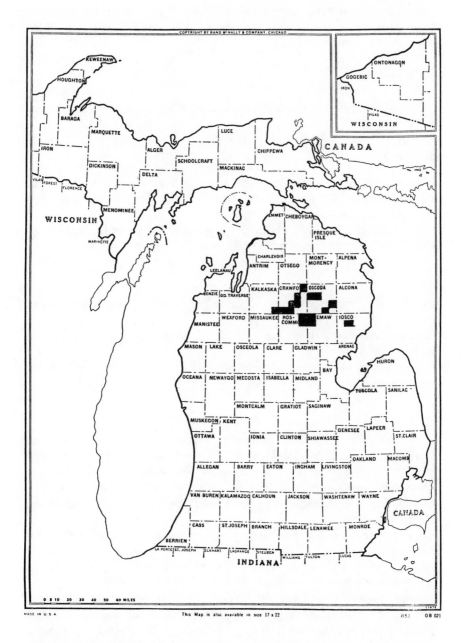

FIGURE 2.   Known Nesting Range of Kirtland's Warbler, 1978–1982.
Black rectangle = 6 mi or 9.7 km per square

emphasized that females were not found with any of the males discussed above. There is, as yet, no evidence that the birds are breeding outside the Lower Peninsula of Michigan.

Fall Migration

The following are fall migration records including last sightings and specimens:

Michigan:

Oscoda County: Luzerne, 9 September 1916, 28 September 1919 (specimens in UMMZ) by M. M. Peet; Mack Lake, 29 September 1975 (sighting) by P. F. Schempf (1976).
Oakland County: Bloomfield Hills, 24 September 1965, one immature male caught, banded, and released by W. P. Nickell (1965).

Ontario:

Essex County: Point Pelee National Park, 2 October 1915 (spec.) by W. E. Saunders (Mayfield 1960).
Haldimand-Norfolk County: Long Point, 31 August 1941 (δ sighting) by H. A. Singer.
Durham County: Pickering, 14 September 1948 (sighting) by D. H. Speirs (personal communication).

Ohio:

Cuyahoga County: Cleveland, 14 October 1886, specimen found under electric light mast by L. M. Davies (1906); Cleveland, 7 October 1934 (two sightings), 2 September 1935 (sighting), 8 September 1940 (sighting), 5 October 1941 (two sightings), 26 September 1943 (sighting) by A. B. Williams (1944); Cleveland, 25 October 1969 (sighting) by J. N. Henderson (Clench 1973).
Fairfield/Perry Counties: Buckeye Lake, September 1928 (sighting) by M. Trautman.
Franklin County: Columbus, Alum Creek, 11 September 1925 (sighting) by E. S. Thomas (1926).
Hamilton County: Cincinnati, Westwood, 27 September 1975, one male specimen (USNM) found dead near a picture window by Suzanne Doerger (This bird was banded as a fledgling on 2 July 1971 at Mack Lake and it nested at Lovells in Crawford County from 1972–1975).
Lorain County: Oberlin, Ironton, 28 August 1902 (sighting) (Clench 1973).
Lucas County: 22 September 1929 (sighting) by L. W. Campbell (1940).

Pennsylvania:

Potter County: Lewisville, 27 September 1964 (sighting) by B. Hurlock (Clench 1973).
Somerset County: Wellersburg, 26 September 1972 (sighting) by P. M. McKenzie (Clench 1973).
Westmoreland County: Rector, Powdermill Nature Reserve, 21 September 1971 to 2 October 1971, immature specimen mist netted, banded, and released by R. C. Leberman (Clench 1973).

Virginia:

Arlington County: Fort Myer, 25 September 1887 (spec.) and 2 October 1887 (sighting) by H. M. Smith and W. Palmer (1888).
Mecklenberg County: Kerr Lake, 1 September 1974 (sighting) by J. M. Potter (1975).

North Carolina:

Pender County: Rocky Point, 2 September 1936, 22 September 1938, 23 September 1941 (sightings) by F. H. Craighill (Craighill 1942; Mayfield 1960).

Tennessee:

Greene County: Greeneville, 28 September 1956 (sighting) by M. Darnell (1956).

South Carolina:

Aiken County: Aiken, 5 October 1960 (sighting) by J. B. Hatcher (1960).
Charleston County: Mt. Pleasant, 29 October 1903 (♂ spec.) by A. T. Wayne (1904); Christ Church Parish, 4 October 1910 (sighting) by A. T. Wayne (1911); Christ Church Parish, 4 October 1910 (sighting) by L. M. Bragg (1912).
Chester County: Chester, 11 October 1888 (♀ spec.) by A. T. Wayne (1910).
Richland County: Eastover, 14 October 1949 (sighting), 1 September 1951 (sighting), and 22 September 1967 (sighting) by A. R. Faver (1949, 1951, 1967).

Florida:

Dade County: Miami, 21 September 1958 (sighting) by R. L. Cunningham and A. Schaffner (Stevenson 1959).
Palm Beach County: West Palm Beach, 2–3 November 1961 (sighting) by V. I. Carmer (Clench 1973); West Palm Beach, 2–3 November 1961, nu-

merous sight records of one individual (Stevenson 1962).

St. John's County: Anastasia Island, 13 October 1935 (spec.) by R. C. Hallman (Sprunt 1963).

St. Lucie County: Fort Pierce, 1 November 1918 (sighting) by H. H. Schroder (1923).

Walkulla County: East Goose Creek, 20 mi west of St. Mark's, 9 September 1919 (sighting) by L. Griscom and J. T. Nichols (Mayfield 1960).

Mexico:

Veracruz: 20 mi south of Veracruz (city), 11 November 1974 (two sightings) by J. Lane (1975).

Bahamas:

Crooked Island: 11, 12, 22 March 1973 (♂ sightings) by B. E. Radabaugh (1974).

New Providence Island: Nassau Airport, 20 August 1970 (sighting) by W. B. Robertson (1971).

Summary

    During the late 1800s Kirtland's Warbler must have been much more common than it is at present. This is indicated by the ease with which collectors obtained the bird in the Bahama Islands and by the number of birds collected across eastern North America from St. Louis, Missouri, to the Spectacle Reef Lighthouse, Michigan. Today the bird is largely restricted to six counties in Michigan's Lower Peninsula, with the majority of the birds found in the four counties of Kalkaska, Crawford, Oscoda, and Ogemaw. The field data show that males reach the breeding grounds between 11–14 May. The females normally arrive less than a week later. The birds may leave the breeding grounds for their southward migration in late August, but most leave in September. Field data also indicate that the species, if given a chance, will take up territory outside the Lower Peninsula of Michigan. If the population of Kirtland's Warblers should increase, its breeding range might well expand into other states and into Canada.

CHAPTER 5

SONG

The first arrival of Kirtland's Warblers in the spring is usually discovered by a male bird singing. The song of the Kirtland's Warbler is exceptionally loud for a warbler and can be heard at a distance of a quarter of a mile. The males begin singing shortly after they arrive on the breeding grounds. Each male seems to have a definite type of song. Warren Faust's study of Kirtland's Warbler vocalizations showed several variations given by different males (personal communication). The most common song type resembles the syllables *'Ter-ter-ter-ter-wee-wee'* (See sonograms by Faust). Males may give this vocalization up to nine times per minute for many minutes. They may continue this pattern, with short pauses, for hours. A second common song type was named the 'Chatter Song' by Faust (personal communication). It resembles the syllables *'Churr-churr-churr-churr'* and is given more softly than the more common song. The rate of vocalization for this song is similar to that of the more common song type. In one region of the Artillery Range North several males sang this 'Chatter Song' simultaneously. Normally, these songs were given from dense stands of small jack pines. We could often identify a male by his song, since the song of each individual has certain distinctive qualities.

At Lovells on 17 June 1978 a single male sang 238 times between 0445 hrs and 0523 hrs EST (sunrise 0500 hrs) or 6.3 songs per minute. He started singing when still down among the denser jack pine branches where he had spent the night. Within 16 min he moved to a perch 3.7 m above ground where he sang for the next 25 minutes. He then dropped again into the thicker branches. His mate was incubating eggs. At Muskrat Lake, also on 17 June 1978, another male was singing at 1039 hrs EST. He sang for one minute on a perch 5.5 m above ground and then dropped to a perch 1.5 m above ground where he sang for three minutes. At 1230 hrs EST he sang for two minutes on a perch 9.1 m above ground and then dropped again into the shorter jack pines. He was silent during 36 minutes of a 58-minute period. At Black River Falls, Jackson County, Wisconsin, one male sang steadily, seven to nine songs per minute, for over half an hour at about 0600 hrs EST. There was no evidence that he had a mate. Some males sang aber-

TABLE 6. Numbers and Locations of Singing Male Kirtland's Warblers.

County	1951	1961	1971	1972	1973	1974	1975	1976	1977	1978	1979	1980	1981	1982
MICHIGAN														
Alcona	4	0	0	0	0	0	0	0	0	0	0	0	0	0
Crawford	142	52	101	101	114	88	90	95	78	74	75	93	72	67
Iosco	74	30	1	0	0	0	0	0	0	2	1	3	3	1
Kalkaska	28	32	0	0	0	0	3	7	11	16	21	38	32	17
Montmorency	43	61	1	0	0	0	0	0	0	0	0	0	0	0
Ogemaw	0	114	47	49	51	35	46	51	62	40	40	46	50	44
Oscoda	103	152	48	48	47	41	35	44	59	62	71	58	67	72
Otsego	0	14	3	0	0	0	0	0	0	0	0	0	0	0
Presque Isle	34	34	0	0	0	0	0	0	0	0	0	0	0	0
Roscommon	4	13	0	0	0	1	4	2	7	2	2	4	8	5
Wexford	0	0	0	2	4	2	1	1	1	0	0	0	0	0
Marquette														1

TABLE 6. Continued

County	1951	1961	1971	1972	1973	1974	1975	1976	1977	1978	1979	1980	1981	1982
Michigan Total	432	502	201	200	216	167	179	200	218	196	210	242	232	207
WISCONSIN														
Jackson										2	1	1		
ONTARIO														
Renfrew									1	1				
QUEBEC														
Gatineau										1				
Total	432	502	201	200	216	167	179	200	219	200	211	243	232	207
Michigan counties	8	9	6	4	4	5	6	6	6	6	6	6	6	7
Michigan sections	91	86	27	27	25	27	31	47	42	36	41	42	46	44
Percent of 1951 Count		116	47	46	50	39	41	46	51	46	49	56	54	48

From Mayfield 1953, 1962a, 1972a, 1973a, 1973b, 1975; Ryel 1976a, 1976b, 1978, 1979a, 1979b, 1980, 1981, 1982.

rant songs. We named one easily identifiable male 'Mr. Odd Song'. Another male uttered a two-syllable song, *'Wee-wee,'* while another had a similar song with three syllables. Neither of these males had mates.

Mayfield (1960) wrote that during a full day count, on 8 June 1945, one male sang 1,229 times. Most of these songs (1,114) were uttered between 0418 hrs and 1100 hrs EST at an average rate of only 2.8 songs per minute. The highest frequency (96) was given during a 15 min period between 0430 hrs and 0445 hrs EST. In contrast, only 115 songs were given between 1100 hrs and 1800 hrs EST. Mayfield (1960) recorded another male which sang 2,212 songs during the entire day of 21 June 1956 (about the 13th day of incubation). The first song was uttered at 0457 hrs EST and the last at 1956 hrs EST (sunrise 0500 hrs, sunset 2025 hrs). This male sang 1,536 songs before noon ($\bar{x}$ = 3.6) and 676 in the afternoon ($\bar{x}$ = 1.7). During the afternoon he sang most often when it was cloudy.

Warren Faust and I heard a thirty-nine-day-old, full-grown fledgling attempt to sing in July 1976. Very shortly thereafter he responded to a recording and was caught in a mist net. The following summer he had a territory of his own 2 km south of the place where he was netted.

During the first few days after arriving on the breeding grounds in the spring, the males frequently sing on perches 1–2 m above ground in the densest growth of jack pines. After a few days, they move up to higher perches. Males who have acquired a mate sing less frequently than unmated males. During late summer some males sing much less than others. At this time, they often become very quiet and retreat into the denser jack pines where they are almost impossible to locate.

Because all or nearly all males sing steadily during early June, Mayfield (1953) organized a group of experienced observers to count the Kirtland's Warblers. These counts were made in June 1951, June 1961 (Mayfield 1962), and June 1971 (Mayfield 1972). The results of these counts are given in Table 6. Although such counts have certain weaknesses, the data they yield provide a basis for calculation of population changes. The singing male count is the best method known to date for making comparable population counts (Table 6). The chief weaknesses of this method are: 1) some males have more than one territory; 2) some males have territories of great size; 3) some males are missed because they are quiet; 4) since the count is generally a one day event, bad weather can effect the amount of singing. Some males are undoubtedly missed when the count is made on a cold, windy, or rainy day. The 1971 count revealed that the Kirtland's Warbler population had been extensively decimated. This was the starting point for the various efforts which have been undertaken to save the species.

The decrease in Kirtland's Warbler numbers shown by the 1971 singing male count indicated that it would be wise to make these counts annually. This has been done every year since 1971. The counts are made on a single

TYPICAL SONGS OF THE KIRTLAND'S WARBLER

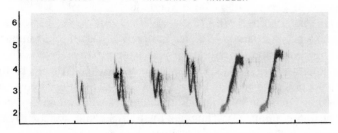

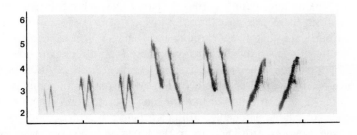

FREQUENCY IN KHz

CHATTER SONGS OF THE KIRTLAND'S WARBLER

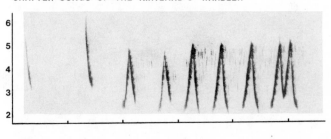

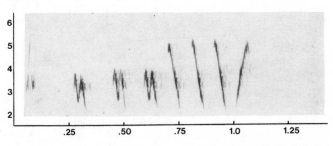

TIME IN SECONDS

day between 5 June and 15 June when nesting activity is at its peak and males are singing regularly. The results of these counts through 1982 are presented in Table 6 (data from Mayfield 1972a, 1973a, 1973b, 1975 and Ryel 1976a, 1976b, 1978, 1979a, 1980, 1981, 1982, personal communication). Since Kirtland's Warbler is nearly always monogamous, the total breeding population for any given year is approximately double the singing male count. Polygyny does occur infrequently and there are times when males do not have mates. For example, in 1978 196 singing males were counted in Michigan but four additional males were found outside Michigan (all apparently unmated). Thus, the total 1978 count was approximately 396 adult birds at the beginning of the breeding season.

The singing male counts during the past 13 years have shown considerable variability. There was an extremely low count in 1974 and it is my belief that a hurricane that swept through the Bahamas in October 1973 was the reason for this low number. However, there is no direct evidence supporting this interpretation. The species has had excellent nesting success since adult Brown-headed Cowbirds have been removed from the breeding grounds and the birds have been found to live for many years, often longer than related species. A sizeable percentage of the Kirtland's Warblers (both banded nestlings and adults) return annually to the breeding grounds. These facts seem to indicate that decreases in numbers must occur outside Michigan where very little is known about the bird.

CHAPTER 6

NESTING HABITAT

General Characteristics

Although jack pine forests are found over extensive regions in Canada from British Columbia to Quebec and in the United States from northern Minnesota eastward, Kirtland's Warbler has been found only in the southern portion of these forests in summer. Up to the present time, it has been found to nest only in a restricted region in the northern part of Michigan's Lower Peninsula. Even in this region the bird is very selective when it chooses a nesting site. The nesting habitat results from fire in mature stands of jack pine under appropriate conditions. If the fire is too intense, jack pine seeds fail to germinate. If the fire is followed by a period of drought, the seeds also fail to germinate. If the stand lacks openings, the warblers often do not use it. In the past, fires produced sufficient habitat for the warblers. Now, however, better roads, fire equipment, and control methods have reduced the extent of these naturally burned regions. The May 1980 fire in Oscoda County which swept through the Mack Lake area destroying 40 homes, as well as extensive jack pine tracts, was an exception.

Kirtland's Warblers first move into an area when the jack pines are at least five or six years old and 0.3 m to 1.8 m tall. The birds prefer to nest in large stands of jack pine over 32.4 ha in size. They prefer stands where there are grassy openings and semi-openings interspersed among dense clumps of jack pines where the trees are about equal in height. Often the openings are scattered with trees connecting the denser stands. Plantations of 40.5 ha have been used successfully by nesting warblers. In these management areas, the jack pines were originally planted 1.2 m apart in rows spaced 1.8 m apart. Ten rows of jack pines were alternated with grassy clearings 15 rows or 27.4 m wide. At Mack Lake red pine plantings have also attracted warblers. These red pine tracts were developed specifically for the warblers and were not planted according to normal forestry management procedures.

Zimmerman (1956: 61) described the jack pine habitat as follows:

"Many plants thrive when the growing season is short, others are well adapted to an existence in sandy soils. Some can withstand repeated

35

severe burning and still survive or reproduce their kind. But the number of species whose tolerances are high enough to successfully cope with all three of these extreme environmental conditions are few. Consequently, the flora of the Michigan Jack Pine barrens is not a rich one. . . .Without the great fires of previous years the jack pine plains of this peninsula probably would not occupy so great an area as they do at present."

Jack pines are the dominant tree in most natural Kirtland's Warbler habitats but in the Damon region, Ogemaw County, jack pines and jack-oaks (*Quercus ellipsoidalis*) are found in about equal proportions. In some regions quaking aspen (*Populus tremuloides*), large-toothed aspen (*Populus grandidentata*), service-berry (*Amelanchier* sp.), pin cherry (*Prunus pensylvanica*), sand cherry (*Prunus pumila*), white pine (*Pinus strobus*), red pine (*Pinus resinosa*), and small willows (*Salix* sp.) occur in small numbers.

The soil in all Kirtland's Warbler nesting regions is some form of Grayling Sand, a fact first pointed out by Harold Wing (verbal communication). This soil is acidic. The jack pine stands in both Ontario and Wisconsin are quite similar and the soil in both cases is fine sand (Paul Aird and Nancy Tilghman, personal communications).

Good ground cover is characteristic of prime Kirtland's Warbler habitat. In general, one or more species of grasses (*Andropogon gerardii, Andropogon scoparius,* and *Danthonia spicata*) mixed with sedge (*Carex pensylvanica*) commonly form the bulk of the ground cover. In other regions blueberry (*Vaccinium angustifolium* and *Vaccinium angustifolium* var. *nigrum*), bearberry (*Arcostaphylos uva-ursi*), wintergreen (*Gaultheria procumbens*), trailing arbutus (*Epigaea repens*), sweet fern (*Comptonia peregrina*), bracken fern (*Pteridium aquilinum*), and blackberry (*Rubus* sp.) are the dominant plants. In the Lovells region, reindeer moss (*Cladonia rangiferina*) is plentifully mixed in with the above named plants. Some of the other plants occurring in Kirtland's Warbler habitat include: harebell (*Campanula rotundifolia*), bird's-foot violet (*Viola pedata*), wood lily (*Lilium philadelphicum*), cinquefoil (*Potentilla* sp.), broad-leafed cow-wheat (*Melampyrum lineare*), St. John's-wort (*Hypericum* sp.) and goldenrod (*Solidago* sp.). These plants do not appear to be essential to the warblers nesting success. Zimmerman (1956) stated that the grass *Andropogon gerardii* in the interior counties was found on 54.5% of burns and 50% of savannas. *Andropogon scoparius* was found on 94% of savannas and 90% of burns and *Carex pensylvanica* was found on all burns and on 96% of savannas.

Plant Surveys

On Kirtland's Warbler territories in different regions the following surveys were made of the number of jack pines, large shrubs and plants:

1) The average number of jack pines in 5 m × 10 m plots through six selected Kirtland's Warbler territories under the leadership of Dr. Paul Aird. Twelve to 14 plots in a row through the heart of the territory were studied (Table 7)

2) On these same plots a survey of all trees and bushes was also made and from this the number of larger plants was estimated on 100 sq m portions of the habitat (Table 8).

3) The number and height of jack pines were recorded for the years 1969–1977 on 94 plots, 6.1 m in diameter with the warbler nest at the center (Table 9).

4) A survey was made at six nests of all plants found in four one-meter square plots with the warbler nest positioned at the intersection of the four squares (Tables 10 and 11).

All these surveys were made immediately following the nesting season.

Summary

The survey of jack pines on seven different nesting regions indicates that Kirtland's Warblers nest where the trees are less than three meters in height although there are often some taller trees on the territory (up to 26 m tall) (Table 7). The presence of other trees and shrubs seems to have little effect on the selection of a nesting site on the territory (Table 8). The 1970 nest location on the Artillery Range North was an exception to the usual location of a nest (Table 9). Here the female built her nest far out in an open area burned three years earlier, the only one I have seen in such a location. Although the territory of this pair included a good area of jack pines where the birds fed, loafed, and slept, the nest was located under grass 56.7 m out in the open. It is also evident that warblers will nest in habitat where some trees reach a height of 6.71 m and where the average height is 4.3 m (Table 9). However, the birds had used these territories for several years and the trees had continued to grow. Blueberry is an almost uniform ground cover for the location of nests, but in some regions grasses are prominent in the habitat (Table 11). The dominant plant growth at 90.5% of 283 nest sites is blueberry and grasses, occurring either separately or in combination (Table 12).

TABLE 7.   Height Distribution and Average dbh of Jack Pines Surrounding Selected Nest Sites (1977).

Region, Section	Nest No.	Height (m) >1	Height (m) 1–2	Height (m) 2–3	Height (m) 3–4	x̄ dbh (cm)	Range in ht. (m)	No. trees
LS-5	0280	77.2	2.7	2.3	2.3	3.4 ± 1.4	1–6	68
LS-5	0293	42.8	0.3	1.6	4.9	4.1 ± 1.1	1–8	77
ARN-8	0284	54.3	12.0	17.5	0.6	—		—
ARN-9	0285	12.9	5.3	9.3	2.5	—		—
ML-13	0296	14.4	41.2	25.6	0.0	3.9 ± 4.7	1–26	142
R-11	0301	7.7	5.3	5.4	0.0	5.9 ± 6.9	1–25	70
Og.22, 27	0306	0.4	1.5	1.9	0.0	5.7 ± 3.5	2–21	96
Overall means		29.9	9.6	9.1	1.4	4.9 ± 5.0	1–26	308

These figures represent the average number of trees in four height classes for twelve 5 × 10 m plots established in the vicinity of each nest location (with the exception of the nest 0306 in Ogemaw County where fourteen 5 × 10 m plots were established). Nests 0280 and 0293 were not included in the determination of overall mean dbh because they occurred in a planted habitat.
dbh = diameter at breast height (1.4 m above ground level)

TABLE 8.   Larger Plants Occurring on Kirtland's Warbler Nesting Territories (1977).

Nest No.:	280	293	284	285	301	296	299	
Region:	LS-5	LS-5	ARN-8	ARN-9	R-11	ML-13	OG-27	
Planted/ Burned:	P	P	NB	NB	NB	NB	NB	Total:
Plots Surveyed	12	12	12	12	12	12	14	86
								Mean
Jack pine	16	14	64 (0.5d)	28	43 (1.8d)	183 (1.7d)	20 (0.9d)	52.3
Service-berry	28	71	101	23	0	0	0	
Pin cherry	8	2.3	0	0	3.0	0	0.1	1.9
Quaking aspen	14	13	0.8	0	0	0	0	3.9
Large-toothed Aspen	13	0	0	0	0	0	0	1.7
Jack-oak	0	0	2.2	10	0.8	0.3	0.1	1.9
Willow	0	0	0.7	0	0	0	0	0.1
Red pine	0	0	0	0	0.2	0	0	0.03
Sweet fern	90	0	0	0	0	0	0	13.0

The sample plots utilized in this study were 5 × 10 m.
P = planted region
NB = natural burn
d = dead jack pines

TABLE 9. Jack Pines in a Kirtland's Warbler Colony (Artillery Range, Crawford County, Michigan)

Year	Age of Burn in Years	No. of Nests Sampled	Average No. Trees in Circle 6.1 m in Diameter with Nest at the Center	Average Height of Trees (m)	Range in Height of Trees (m)	Average Height of Live Jack Pine Closest to Nest (m)	Average Distance from Nest to Closest Live Jack Pine (cm)
			Artillery Range North (Burned in May 1967)				
1970	3	1	1 (dead)				5670.0
1974	7	3	38.0 (8–81)	1.32 ± 0.30	0.61–1.52	1.01 ± 0.45	20.0
1975	8	4	18.0 (13–20)	1.53 ± 0.51	0.45–3.35	1.23 ± 0.52	23.1
1976	9	7	22.7 (3–42)	1.63 ± 0.52	0.31–3.35	1.60 ± 0.48	56.8
1977	10	6	18.0 (4–28)	1.75 ± 0.59	0.31–3.35	1.82 ± 0.33	52.5
Mean		4.2	22.6 (3–81)	1.57 ± 1.07	0.31–3.35	1.55 ± 0.46	38.1
			Artillery Range South (Burned August 1955)				
1969	14	3	16.7 (9–22)	2.24 ± 0.87	1.22–4.88	2.63 ± 1.22	29.2
1970	15	16	17.4 (3–55)	3.12 ± 1.21	0.31–10.68	2.88 ± 1.07	41.1
1971	16	10	10.1 (5–25)	3.56 ± 1.14	0.61–6.40	3.62 ± 1.07	42.5
1972	17	20	9.7 (4–15)	3.36 ± 1.11	0.31–5.79	3.27 ± 0.96	35.9
1973	18	8	7.6 (4–12)	3.54 ± 1.38	0.31–6.40	3.50 ± 1.88	38.6
1974	19	12	16.2 (7–30)	3.41 ± 0.84	0.91–6.71	3.63 ± 1.36	45.2
1975	20	3	6.3 (4–10)	4.30 ± 1.28	1.52–5.49	2.16	28.5
1976	21	1	10.0	4.50	3.35–4.88	3.40	62.0
Mean		9.1	12.4 (3–55)	3.37 ± 1.04	0.31–10.68	3.21 ± 1.23	39.6

TABLE 10.   Plant Codes Utilized in Table 11

Code	Common Name	Scientific Name
01	jack pine	*Pinus banksiana*
02	red pine	*Pinus resinosa*
03	jack-oak	*Quercus ellipsoidalis*
04	sweet fern	*Comptonia peregrina*
05	bearberry	*Arctostaphylos uva-ursi*
06	trailing arbutus	*Epigaea repens*
07	strawberry	*Fragaria* sp.
08	blueberry	*Vaccinium angustifolium*
		Vaccinium angustifolium var. *nigrum*
		Vaccinium brittoni
09	sand cherry	*Prunus pumila*
010	bracken fern	*Pteridium aquilinum*
011	wintergreen	*Gaultheria procumbens*
012	big bluestem grass	*Andropogon gerardii*
013	little bluestem grass	*Andropogon scoparius*
014	oatgrass	*Danthonia spicata*

Other plants found in some of these nest regions were: harebell (*Campanula rotundifolia*), service-berry (*Amelanchier* sp.), wild rose (*Rosa pumila*), dewberry (*Rubus canadensis*), king-devil hawkweed (*Hieracium aurantiacum*), dwarf dandelion (*Krigia* sp.), reindeer moss (*Cladonia rangiferina*), bird's-foot violet (*Viola pedata*), Pennsylvania sedge (*Carex pensylvanica*), pin cherry (*Prunus pensylvanica*), and goldenrod (*Solidago* sp.).

Four one-meter-square plots were established around each nest site, with the nest located in the intersection of the plots. Plants without code numbers do occur in the vicinity of nests, but none was found in the sample plots.

TABLE 11. Average Stem Counts of Plants in One-Meter-Square Plots Around Kirtland's Warbler Nests (1977).

| | Region/Nest Number | | | | | | |
| | ARN-9 | | MaL | | ML-13 | | Overall |
	0284	0285	0308	0268	0295	0296	Mean
Plant codes:							
01	5.0	3.0	0.3	2.3	3.0	2.3	2.65
02				0.5			0.08
03		4.5		0.3			0.8
04	47.8	80.3			9.3	10.3	24.6
05		51.0		1.3	23.8	6.5	13.8
06		1.5		0.5			0.3
07		8.0					1.3
08	106.3	53.5	133.5	32.5	71.3	96.0	82.0
09		16.3	2.5			12.0	5.1
010				30.3		17.3	7.9
011				210.3		60.5	45.1
012*	36%	95.5%		some	34.8%		—
013	86.0				8.0		16.7
014							

Four one-meter-square plots were delineated around each nest, with the nest located at the intesection of the plots (after the nests were terminated). Figures given above are the average number of stems in these four plots for each nest. Plant codes are given in Table 10. *Where individual stems could not be counted, the percentage of ground cover within the one-meter-square was estimated.

TABLE 12.   Dominant Ground Cover Around Kirtland's Warbler Nests.

Dominant Plant Around Nest	Artillery Range	Lovells Mgmt. Area	Other Regions	Total	Percent
Blueberry	58	13	22	93	32.9
Big bluestem grass, little bluestem grass, oatgrass	11	39	9	59	20.8
Blueberry, grasses (about equal cover)	41	30	17	88	31.1
Sweet fern, grasses	1	3	1	5	1.8
Blueberry, grasses, bracken fern	6	2	8	16	5.7
Blueberry, sweet fern	2	—	2	4	1.4
Sand cherry, grasses	—	2	—	2	0.7
Bracken fern (dead)	1	—	4	5	1.8
Bearberry	—	—	2	2	0.7
Bearberry, bracken fern, blueberry, sweet fern	1	1	1	3	1.0
Sedges	1	1	—	2	0.7
Sheep-laurel	—	—	1	1	0.4
Other associations	2	—	1	3	1.0
Totals	124	91	68	283	100.0

CHAPTER 7

TERRITORIAL ESTABLISHMENT AND BEHAVIOR

Establishment of Territories by First-Year Males

Twelve of 27 male Kirtland's Warblers which were banded as nestlings were found the following year within 1.6 km of the nest in which they hatched ($\bar{x} = 0.0981 \pm .53$ km). Thirteen of 27 males were found the following year in a region other than the one in which they hatched at an average distance of 20.4 ± 12.6 km. Considering these males in a group, the average distance between where the male hatched and where he was found the following year was 11.1 ± 13.3 km (range, 97 m to 45 km) (Table 13, Figures 3, 4, and 5). The other two males were found considerable distances from where they hatched in Michigan. One male, originally banded at Lovells on 24 June 1974, was found in 1978, 101 km north of Ottawa, Canada, a distance of 676 km from where he fledged. The other male, originally banded at the Artillery Range South on 29 June 1972, was found in June 1978 at Black River Falls, Wisconsin, a distance of 579 km from where it hatched (Chamberlain and McKeating 1978; Tilghman 1979).

Six males that fledged on the Artillery Range South were found the following year in the 1967 burn on the Artillery Range North, a distance of 1.38 km to 3.1 km. The Artillery Range South burned on 19 August 1955 while the Artillery Range North burned in early May 1967. Thus, the Artillery Range North had jack pines that were younger and smaller than those on the Artillery Range South and better ground vegetation, making it a more attractive habitat to the warblers (Figure 4). This tendency to breed in younger stands than those in which the warblers hatched was also apparent when all 25 males were considered as a group. One-year-old males tended to settle first in young stands of jack pines, perhaps because they experienced less competition there. Stands in which these 25 males hatched had an average age, based on the date of the fire which created them, of 14.9 ± 3.4 years (range, 9 years to 22 years). Trees on these areas commonly reached 6.7 m in height. In contrast, stands where these males established territories during

TABLE 13. Histories of Returned Male Kirtland's Warblers Banded as Nestlings.

Band Number (his mates)	Date Fledged	Nest Location	Father	Mother	Years Discovered on Study Areas — Nest Number and Number of Nestlings Fledged	Age in Years[1]	Distance Moved and Area[2]
1. 75-36698 (NB)	7/01/69	ARS-16 69-N6	70-94220	75-36687	1972; 1973; — ; —	4	43 km MaL
2. 116-24462 (73:820-89201) (74:81-58978)	7/02/71	MaL	—	—	1972 NNF; 1973 N-2; 1974 N-2, N-38; 1975 N-15; — ; —	4*	45 km LMA-5
3. 61-24166 (NB)	6/30/70	ARS-16 70-N5	112-09428	61-24186	1971 NNF; 1972 NNF, 4 yf; 1973 N-32, 5 yf; 1974 NNF; 1975 N-18, 1 yf	5	17 km PC
4. 80-57180 (820-89205)	6/26/71	ARS-16 71-N11	80-57186	61-24171	1972 NNF; 1973 N-12, 5 yf; 1974 — ; —	2	15.3 km LMA-5
5. 81-58909 (820-89263)	6/12/72	ARS-17 72-N12	61-24183	75-36690	1973 N-30, 4 yf; 1974 NNF; 1975 NNF; 1976 NNF; 1977 NFF	5	1609 m ARN-8
6. 81-58913 (81-58978)	6/23/72	LMA-5 72-N19	81-58934	81-58935	1973 N-20, 2 yf; 1974–1980 NF; 1981 ARN-N, 5 yf	9	460 m LMA-5; 14.5 km ARN-8
7. 81-58930 (74:81-58914) (75:81-58914) (76:830-20555) (77:880-52640) (78:860-40320)	6/25/72	LMA-5 72-N20	81-58936	61-24179	1973 NNF; 1974 N-22, N-43, 2 yf, LMA; 1975 N-17, N-36, 4 yf, LMA; 1976 N-9, N-31, 5 yf, LMA; 1977 N-4, 5 yf, LMA; 1978 N-1, 5 yf, LMA	6	1208 m LMA-6
8. 81-58942	6/26/72	AR-17 72-N18	—	81-58974	1973 NNF; 1974 NNF, 5 yf; — ; —	2	1464 m ARN-8
9. 81-58944 (NB)	6/25/72	ARS-16 72-N24	81-58854	80-57193	1973, 5 yf; 1974, 5 yf; — ; —	2	21 km ML-13

TABLE 13. Continued

	Band Number (his mates)	Date Fledged	Nest Location	Father	Mother	Years Discovered on Study Areas — Nest Number and Number of Nestlings Fledged							Age in Years[1]	Distance Moved and Area[2]
						1973	1974	1975	1976	1977	1978	1979		
10.	81-58947 (NF)	6/25/72	ARS-16 72-N24	81-58854	80-57193	NNF	NNF	NNF	NNF	—	—	—	4	1609 m ARN-8
11.	81-58952 (NF)	6/29/72	ARS-15 72-N14	—	—	NNF	NNF	NNF	—	—	—	—	3	3.1 km ARN-9
12.	81-58962 (73 & 75: NNF) (74,76,78: NB) (77:880-52613)	6/28/72	ARS-16 72-N4	61-24195	81-58943	NNF	N-19 4 yf	NNF yf	N-16 4 yf	N-6 5 yf	N-12 yf	NNF	7	1380 m ARN-9
13.	81-58977 (none banded)	6/26/72	LMA-5 72-N29	81-58976	81-58975	0 yf LMA-5	NNF LMA-5	NNF	2 yf KL-19	—	—	—	4	1:395 m 2:10 km
14.	81-58979 (73-76: NB) (77:880-52641)	6/26/72	LMA-5 72-N29	81-58976	81-58975	NNF	4 yf	N-26 4 yf	N-24 5 yf	N-19 4 yf	—	—	5	21 km ML-13
15.	820-89206 (74:110-09018) (76:860-40308) (77:860-40328) (75,78: NB) (79, ?)	6/28/73	LMA-5 73-N2	116-24662	820-89201	N-35 0 yf ML-13	N-35,37 8 yf	N-8,32 7 yf LMA-5	N-30 LMA-5 2 yf	N-17 yf LMA-5	NNF LMA-5	NNF	6	1:21 km 2:21 km ML-13 LMA-5
16.	820-89211 (74:830-20518) (75:820-89252) (75:830-20532) (2 mates 1975)	6/28/73	LMA-5 73-N10	81-58936	61-24179	—	N-23 N-42 9 yf	N-10 N-35,37 8 yf	—	—	—	—	2	1183 m LMA-6
17.	820-89224 (860-40320)	6/28/73	ARS-16 73-N5	820-89202	61-24172	—	NNF	N-5 5 yf	NNF	NNF	—	—	4	15.3 km LMA-5
18.	820-89230 (74,75:820-89288) (76:860-40328) (77,78,79: NB)	7/01/73	LMA-5 73-N11	820-89214	81-58935	—	N-16 4 yf	N-12 4 yf	N-14 0 yf	N-3 0 yf	NNF	NNF	6	395 m LMA-5
19.	830-20541 (860-40370)	6/24/74	ARS-17 73-N27	—	—	—	—	N-27 0 yf	N-27 0 yf	—	—	—	2	12.9 km NDRR

TABLE 13. Continued

Band Number (his mates)	Date Fledged	Nest Location	Father	Mother	Years Discovered on Study Areas — Nest Number and Number of Nestlings Fledged						Age in Years[1]	Distance Moved and Area[2]
20. 830-20584 (NF)	7/05/74	LMA-5 74-N14	820-89230	820-89288	1975 NNF	1976 NNF	—	—	—		2	19.3 km KL-19
21. 830-20589 (NB)	7/05/74	ARS-16 74-N18	820-89202	81-58974	1975 NF	1976 N-14 5 yf	1977 N-7 0 yf	—	—		3	1182 m ARN-9
22. 850-72548 (NB)	6/24/74	MaL	—	—	1975 NNF	1976 N-22 5 yf	—	—	—		2	28.2 km KL-20
23. 850-72503 (116-24635)	6/21/74	ML-13	—	—	1975 NF	1976 NF	1977 N-20 3 yf	—	—		3	97 m ML-13
24. 860-40313 (NB)	6/18/76	ARN-8 76-N16	81-58962	—	1977 NNF	—	—	—	—		1	2.8 km KL-20
25. 860-40316 (77:81-58948) (78,81: NB)	6/24/76	ARN-8 76-N14	830-20589	—	1977 N-3 2 yf	1978 NNF	1979 N-8 0 yf	1980 NNF	1981 NNF		5	790 m ARN-9
26. 81-58970 (NF)	6/29/72	ARS-17 72-N16	61-58987	61-24178	1973 NF	1974 NF	1975 NF	1976 NF	1977 NF	1978 NNF	6	579 km Wisconsin
27. 830-20521 (NF)	6/24/74	LMA-5 74-N6	830-20519	830-20524	1975 NF	1976 NF	1977 NF	1978 NNF	—	—	4	676 km Quebec

*116-24662 was killed by flying into a picture window at Westwood, Cincinnati, Ohio on 27 September 1975.

NF = Bird alive but not found; NNF = Nest not found; NB = Female not found; yf = Young fledged; DF = Date fledged;

Location codes refer to study area and section numbers; mates are given in parentheses below the band numbers of males.

[1]Age when last seen

[2]Distance between natal nest site and breeding nest site or distance between breeding nest sites.

Tables 13 and 14 include seven birds of known age banded by Bruce Radabaugh and Craig Orr which appeared on the author's study areas. These birds are not included in Table 1.

their first breeding season had an average age of 9.8 years (range, 6 years to 15 years) and the trees on these areas seldom exceeded 3.8 m in height. The Wilcoxon matched-pair rank sum procedure was used to statistically compare the ages of stands in which the males hatched with the ages of stands in which they were found the following year. Stands in which males bred were significantly younger than stands in which they hatched (W = 244.5; P = 0.0012).

Jack pines were planted at the Lovells Management Area in 1958 and 1960. Nine males banded as nestlings in this region were found during later years (Table 13, Figure 5). Five remained at Lovells and were found their first year an average of 728 ± 428 m from where they hatched (range, 395 m to 1,208 m). Three of these males banded as nestlings at Lovells bred on two different regions during their lifetime. One of these birds (820-89206) first bred at Muskrat Lake, Oscoda County, for two years and then returned to breed at Lovells, Crawford County, for the next four years. Another male (81-58977) bred two years at Lovells and was later found at Kyle Lake, 18.4 km to the south. A third male (81-58930) bred in the northern part of the Lovells region for three years and then moved to the southern part of the same region, a distance of 1.2 km. A fourth male (81-58913) banded in 1972 was found nesting the following year 460 m from its birthplace. He was not found again until 1981 when he was located on the Artillery Range North, 14.5 km to the south. As previously mentioned, one male banded in 1974 was found in Quebec in late May 1978.

Once first-year males established territories, they normally returned to the same region in subsequent years. In some cases, jack pines increased in size and height during this period of several years to the point where they were no longer attractive to new males. Thus, no new males moved in to replace old birds when they disappeared. Twenty-five males banded as nestlings returned the following year. Of these, 24 returned during two or more seasons (Table 13). Twenty of these males returned to the same general vicinity each year and four bred in two different regions.

Territorial Defense

Immediately upon arrival on the breeding grounds most male Kirtland's Warblers select and defend their territories. Often violent battles occur along territorial boundaries. On occasion, two, three, or more birds may be involved. The birds make bodily contact in midair and flutter with breasts and feet against each other. They come to the ground briefly and then resume the airborne chase. The Kirtland's Warbler, in many cases, uses song as a mechanism for territorial defense. Birds on a disputed territory will sing and chase each other through the jack pine branches until respective territories have been established. The original owner usually pursues the intruder. When

TABLE 14. Histories of Returned Female Kirtland's Warblers Banded as Nestlings.

#	Band No. (mates band)	Date Fledged	Nest Location	Father	Mother	Years Discovered on Study Areas — Nest No. and No. of Young Fledged							Last Seen Age (yrs)	Last Seen Area Section
1.	110-09079 (mate NB)	7/22/67	MaL	—	—	1968 NF	1969 NF	1970 —	1971 NF	1972 N-11, 0 yf	1973 NF	1974 N-15, 0 yf	7	43 km ARS-16
2.	116-24628 (70:61-24180)	7/30/68	MaL	—	—	1969 NF	1970 N-1, 3 yf						2	43 km ARS-17
3.	116-24635 (77:850-72503)	6/25/70	MaL	—	—	1971 NF	1972 MaL, 5 yf	1973 NF	1975 NF	1976 NF	1977 N-20, 3 yf		7	27 km ML-13
4.	850-72516 (mate NB)	6/23/74	PC	—	—	1975 N-33, 5 yf							1	17 km ARN-9
5.	81-58948 (73:56-57414) (77:860-40316)	6/25/72	ARS-16 N-24	81-58854	80-57193	1973 ARS, 5 yf	1974 NF	1975 NF	1976 NF	1977 ARN-9, 2 yf			5	2 km ARS-15, ARN-9
6.	81-58914 (74:81-58930) (75:81-58930)	6/23/72	LMA-5 N-19	81-58934	81-58935	1973 NF	1974 N-43, 2 yf	1975 N-17, N-36, 4 yf					3	1.3 km LMA-6
7.	81-58968 (820-89281)	6/25/72	LMA-5 N-28	81-59000	81-58999	1973 N-31, 1 yf							1	798 m LMA-5
8.	81-58978 (73:81-58913) (74:116-24662)	6/26/72	LMA-5 N-29	81-58976	81-58975	1973 N-20, 2 yf	1974 N-2, 38, 5 yf						2	183 m LMA-5
9.	820-89228 (81-59000)	6/28/73	LMA-5 N-11	820-89214	81-58935	1974 N-13, 5 yf							1	968 m LMA-5
10.	820-89229	6/28/73	LMA-5	820-	81-	1975	1976						3	85 m LMA-5

TABLE 14. Continued

No.	Band No. (mates band)	Date Fledged	Nest Location	Her Father	Her Mother	Years Discovered on Study Areas — Nest No. and No. of Young Fledged						Last Seen Age (yrs)	Last Seen Area Section
	(76:860-40329)		N-11	89214	58935	NF	—	—	NF	N-10 / 4 yf	—		LMA-5
11.	820-89252 (75:820-89211)	7/01/73	LMA-5 N-8	—	—	1974 NF	1975 N-10, 35 / 4 yf	—	—	—	—	2	945 m LMA-6
12.	820-89269 (830-20539)	7/09/73	ARS-16 N-7	—	—	1974 N-17 / 4 yf	—	—	—	—	—	1	1.6 km ARN-8
13.	820-89288 (74,75:820-89230)	7/27/73	LMA-5 N-33	81-58936	61-24179	1974 N-14 / 4 yf	1975 N-16 / 4 yf	—	—	—	—	2	229 m LMA-5
14.	830-20517 (75:rt.banded) (76,77:860-40390)	6/24/74	LMA-5 N-2	116-24662	81-58978	1975 N-32 / 4 yf	1976 N-1 / N-28	1977 N-18	—	—	—	3	743 m LMA-5
15.	830-20530 (75,76,77:860-40301)	6/22/74	LMA-5 N-24	830-20585	61-24179	1975 N-9 / 4 yf	1976 N-7 / 5 yf	1977 N-1, 14 / 2 yf	—	—	—	3	715 m LMA-5
16.	830-20532 (820-89211)	6/22/74	LMA-5 N-24	830-20585	61-24179	1975 N-37 / 4 yf	—	—	—	—	—	1	179 m LMA-5
17.	830-20555 (76:81-58930)	6/27/74	LMA-6 N-23	820-89211	830-20518	1975 NF	1976 N-9, 31 / 5 yf	—	—	—	—	2	1.1 km LMA-5
18.	860-40330 (860-40352)	6/23/75	LMA-5 N-6	830-20519	61-24179	1976 N-20 / 5 yf	—	—	—	—	—	1	446 m LMA-5
19.	860-40326 (77:860-40393) (78: NB)	6/19/76	LMA-5 N-7	860-40301	830-20530	1977 N-5, 27 / 0 yf	1978 N-11 / 5 yf	—	—	—	—	2	1) 917 m LMA-5 2) 14 km ARN-9
20.	860-40343 (mate NB)	6/25/76	LMA-5 N-21	—	—	1977 N-11, 28 / 2 yf	—	—	—	—	—	1	795 m LMA-5

See Table 13 for explanation of codes.

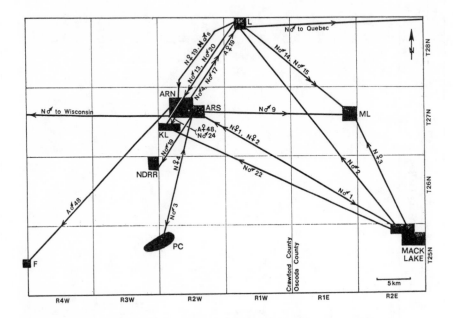

FIGURE 3.   Movements in Nest Locations of Kirtland's Warblers Among
Different Nesting Regions.
N = Movement from natal region to region of first nesting
A = Movement of an adult bird to a different breeding area
ML = Muskrat Lake
L = Lovells Management Area
ARN = Artillery Range North
ARS = Artillery Range South
NDRR = North Down River Road
PC = Pere Cheney
KL = Kyle Lake
F = Fletcher Burn

a strange male enters the territory of a resident male he remains in the lower
jack pine branches in an alert, quiet, and watchful state. If the intruder begins singing, signifying that he is attempting to establish a territory, a con-
frontation with the owner ensues. Kirtland's Warblers defend their territory
well into the summer, but by late July most territorial fighting ceases.
   Males often defend their territories against other species of birds, especially if these birds approach a nest. Even the female Kirtland's Warbler
will exhibit defensive behavior and will chase such intruders as other Kirtland's Warblers, Chipping Sparrows (*Spizella passerina*), Vesper Sparrows
(*Pooecetes gramineus*), Black-capped Chickadees (*Parus atricapillus*), and

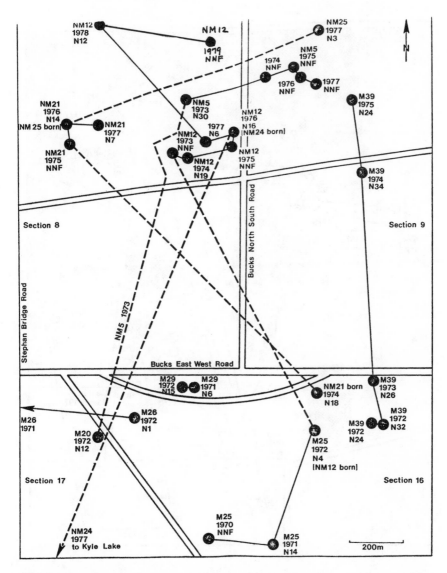

FIGURE 4.   Nest Locations of Male Kirtland's Warblers on the Artillery Range and Nest Locations of Their Male Offsprings.

Black circle = Nest location

M = Males banded as adults

NM = Males banded as nestlings

Code numbers = Birds described in Table 13

Dashed line = Distance between natal nest and first nesting site

Solid line = Distance between nest sites of adult males

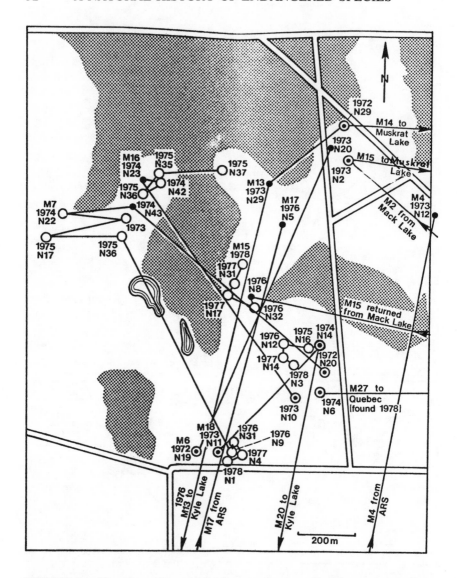

FIGURE 5.   Nest Locations of Males on the Lovells Management Area.
Year and nest number are given next to each nest site. All males included
in this figure were banded as nestlings. Stippling indicates areas of mature
jack pines too large for nesting habitat.
Open circle with dot = Natal nest of males banded as nestlings
Black circle = First nest site
Open circle = Subsequent nest sites
Code numbers = Birds described in Table 13

Nashville Warblers (*Vermivora ruficapilla*) away from the nest site. Both male and female warblers will flutter a few centimeters above Blue Jays (*Cyanocitta cristata*), thirteen-lined ground squirrels (*Citellus tridecemlineatus*), red squirrels (*Tamiasciurus hudsonicus*), and other small potential predators that come too close to their nest. One or both of the warblers will often go into a distraction display, fluttering just above ground level in front of these enemies or a human. Some females are so protective that they will peck a person's fingers if the vegetation above the nest is touched. Other females, however, are so shy that they will leave the region when the nest is discovered. I once caught a female at her nest and she subsequently deserted her five eggs. If a recorded Kirtland's Warbler song is played on an established territory, the male will arrive immediately to drive the intruder away which makes it quite easy to capture males in mist-nets.

Changes in Territorial Size

One method of quantifying shifts in territorial locations has been to measure the distance between the nests of males that return to a region in subsequent years (Figures 3, 4, 5, 7, 8). Four males did not return to their original breeding regions, but established new territories in different regions. One male which bred on the Artillery Range South, Crawford County, was found the following year on the Fletcher Burn, Kalkaska County. Another male was banded as a nestling at Lovells, Crawford County, and returned to breed at Lovells. However, he relocated to the Kyle Lake region during a subsequent year. A third male banded as a nestling at Lovells, Crawford County, bred at Muskrat Lake, Oscoda County, for two years and then returned to nest for four years at Lovells. A fourth male nested at Lovells, Crawford County, during its first breeding season and was not found again until 1981 when he nested on the Artillery Range North. The distances between the different breeding territories of these four males were 19.7 km, 21.0 km, 13.8 km, and 36.2 km respectively. If these four records are omitted, the average distance between nests of males breeding more than one year was 215 ± 251 m (range, 16 m to 1,609 m). These figures were derived from observations of 39 males involving 109 measurements. One of these males lost his original territory to fire just prior to the 1967 breeding season, then established a new territory 1,609 m from his old territory.

Fifty-eight similar records were obtained for 28 female warblers (Figures 6 and 9). The average distance between successive nests during different years was 1,205 m (range, 15.9 m to 25,700 m). Only four of these females nested in two different regions. If these four extreme records are omitted, the average distance becomes 263 ± 447 m (range, 15.9 m to 3,031.5 m). The four extreme distances were 15.3 km, 2.0 km, 25.8 km, and 9.7 km.

Mayfield (1960) pointed out that Kirtland's Warbler territories are very

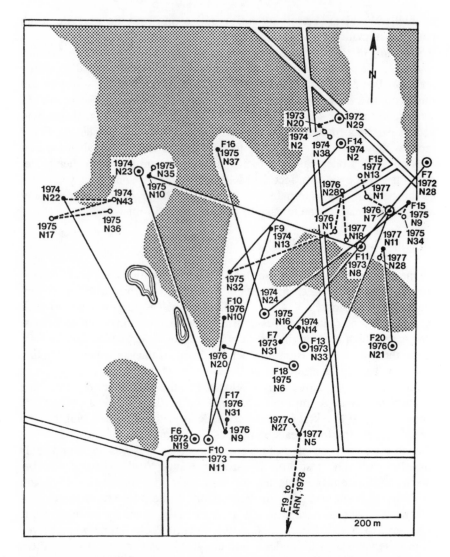

FIGURE 6.   Nest Locations of Females on the Lovells Management Area. All females included in this figure were banded as nestlings. See Figure 5 for explanation of symbols.
Code numbers = Birds described in Table 14

large compared to those of most other warblers. New arrivals seldom establish territories adjacent to other males. A single male may be the sole occupant of as much as 12 ha of suitable habitat, but the entire territory is seldom utilized.

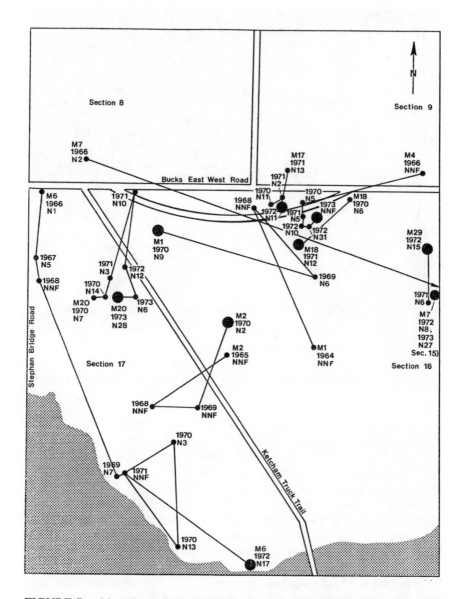

FIGURE 7.   Nest Locations of Males on the Artillery Range. All males included in this figure were banded as adults. Sections 8, 9, 16, and 17 on this map burned in August 1955. Sections 8 and 9 burned again in May 1967.

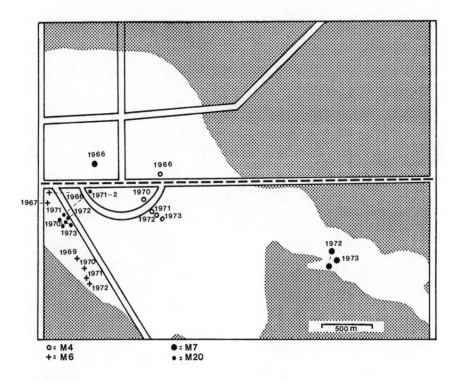

o: M4   ●: M7
+: M6   ● : M20

FIGURE 8.   Returns of Males Banded as Adults to the Artillery Range.

The first four pairs of Kirtland's Warblers known to breed on the Artillery Range South were found by Douglas Middleton and Fenn Holden in 1961, six years after the 1955 fire (personal communication). The warbler was not studied in detail on this territory until 1966 (Figures 10–22). At this time, their territories were plotted on an aerial photograph and the average territorial size was shown to be 7.9 ha. In 1969 only the western half of the Artillery Range South was studied. Forty-nine singing males were found on the western half, thus there could have been more than 80 males on the entire ARS region. In 1971, 62 males were counted on the entire Artillery Range South. Available habitat consisted of 486 ha, most of which was occupied by Kirtland's Warbler. Each pair could have averaged 7.84 ha of land, but if actual territorial sizes were determined the average per pair was 6.08 ha. A summary of these data is presented in Table 15. After 1971 less habitat was used and territorial sizes increased. The last four males were found on the Artillery Range South in 1977 when many of the trees exceeded 5–6 m in height.

Following the May 1967 fire, Kirtland's Warblers were not found again on the Artillery Range North until 1971. At this time a female which had lost a nest on the Artillery Range South moved into the grassy habitat and built an atypical nest under a fallen, dead jack pine located 57 m north of the forested edge of the Artillery Range South (Figure 15). Jack pines in the grassy area were 5 cm in height. In 1972 a banded male moved into the Artillery Range North although no nest was found. By 1973 eight males had taken up territories on the Artillery Range North and their numbers increased almost yearly until 1980 (Table 16; Figures 10–22). During 1980, when the peak number of males was found, about 195 ha of habitat was available or 3.98 ha per pair.

The peak years for Kirtland's Warblers in these two regions (ARS and ARN) were 14 years and 13 years, respectively, following the fires. After that time the populations began to decline. The last time the Artillery Range South was used came 22 years after the fire. When populations reach low numbers it is difficult to estimate actual territorial sizes accurately. The males

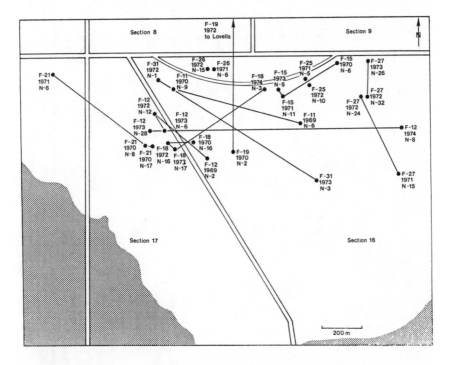

FIGURE 9.   Nest Locations of Females on the Artillery Range. All females included in this figure were banded as adults.

TABLE 15. Size of Kirtland's Warbler Territories (Artillery Range South, T27N, R2W, Crawford County, Michigan)

Year	Usable Area (ha)	Size of Burn (ha)	Study Area Occupied (ha)	Number of Singing Males Observed	Average Size of	
					Complete Region Used (ha)[1]	Territory Mean Size Plotted on Aerial Photograph (ha)
1961	647	933	—	4	—	Unlimited
1966	728	933	348	44	7.91	11.0
1967	486	486	227	33	6.89	8.0
1968	486	486	—	21	—	—
1969	486	486	202	49	4.12	4.12
1970	486	486	267	35	7.63	7.63
1971	486	486	486	62	7.84	6.08
1972	486	486	486	53	9.17	6.31
1973	486	486	486	49	9.92	6.86
1974	324	486	486	26	12.46	6.48
1975	324	486	324	25	12.95	8.48
1976	324	486	324	7	42.29	Unlimited
1977	324	486	324	4	81.0	Unlimited
1978	324	486	324	0	—	—

Total males studied on burn   386

Average Territory Size   10.68   8.42

[1] 1961, 1968, 1976–1978 not in averages

rarely used the extreme borders of their territories. Field observations seem to indicate that Kirtland's Warblers prefer to nest in close proximity to each other forming a colony of sorts. Extensive regions of suitable habitat observed in the field are devoid of warblers. Yet other areas of suitable habitat may support a dense population of warblers e.g. the Artillery Range South during the period 1966–1973. As the jack pines increase in height, the lower branches die and the ground cover disappears. When the trees reach this stage, fewer warblers establish territories in the area. They prefer to nest

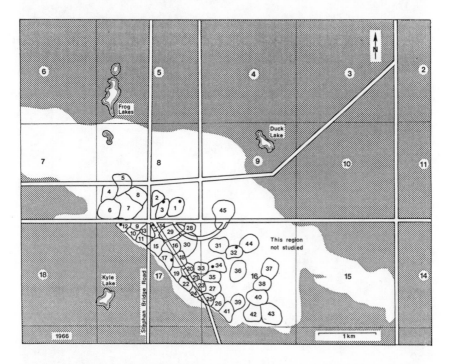

FIGURES 10–21.   Kirtland's Warbler Territories on the Artillery Range. These figures show the gradual movement of warblers into the Artillery Range North which burned in 1967 and a concomitant decrease of warblers on the Artillery Range South which burned in 1955. Clear portions of the maps outline the original August 1955 burn. The clear area north of the dashed line (after 1966) was burned again in May 1967. Territories, which are approximate, were defined by observing the activities of singing males. Stippling indicates mature jack pine forest that did not burn in either 1955 or 1967.

Black circles = Nest locations
Open circle with dot = Active cowbird trap (1972–1978)

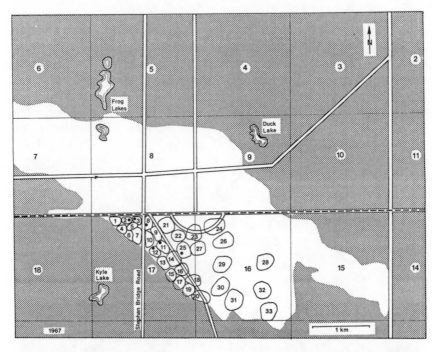

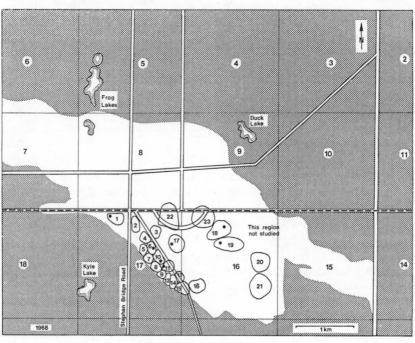

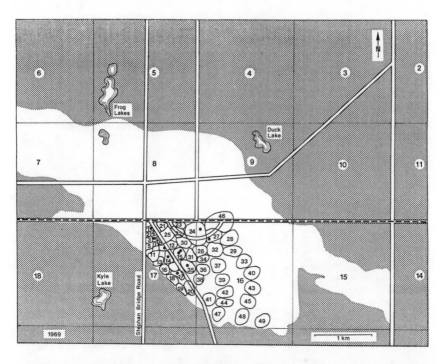

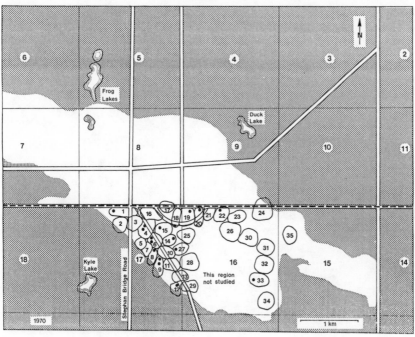

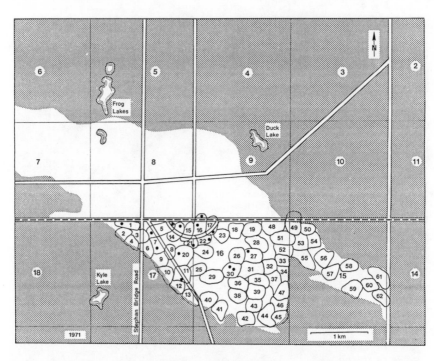

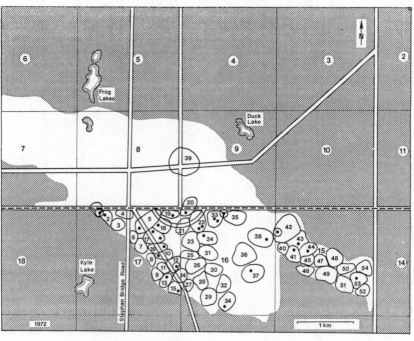

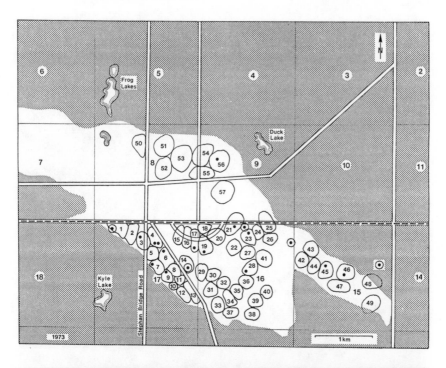

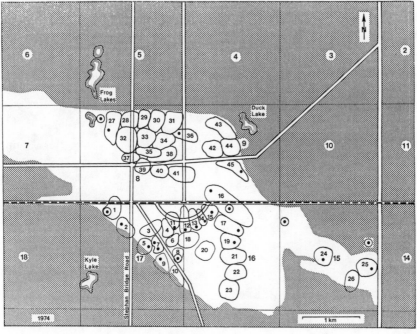

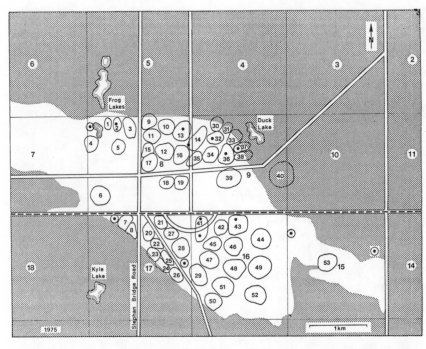

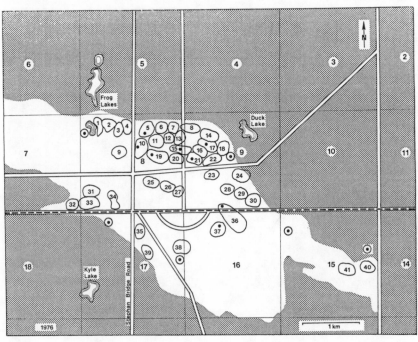

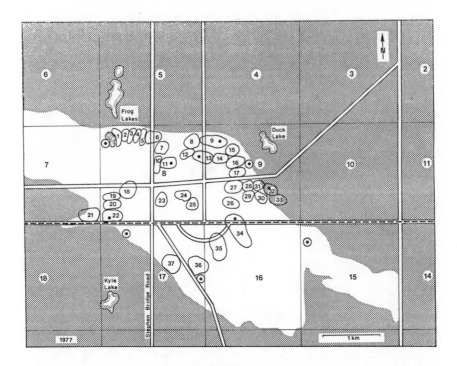

among younger and smaller jack pines where there is lush ground cover and where the lower jack pine branches from each tree reach or nearly reach those of neighboring trees.

Since Kirtland's Warblers nest only in stands of small jack pines, the effective lifetime of a particular stand as warbler habitat depends on the rate of growth of the trees and on the amount of ground cover which in turn depends on edaphic and climatic conditions. Jack pines in the region of Petawawa, Ontario, where Paul Aird found a singing male Kirtland's Warbler in 1977, were much more spindly than those in Michigan. The distance between the branches on each trunk indicated that growth had been much more rapid than is normally seen in Michigan jack pine stands. Both the amount of precipitation and the soil type affect the rate of growth of jack pines; variations in soil and moisture can result in differential growth rates on different tracts. Nearly all jack pine colonies in Michigan are found where Grayling Sand is the dominant soil. Regions where the birds were found in Ontario and Wisconsin also had sandy soil.

In 1961 I found a lone male Kirtland's Warbler northwest of Loon Lake, Oscoda County, in a 3 ha stand of small jack pines. Douglas Middleton found an area only 4.9 ha in size occupied by the species (personal communication). Sometimes two or three males will settle in regions of 20–25

TABLE 16. Size of Kirtland's Warbler Territories (Artillery Range
North, T27N, R2W, Sections 7, 8, and 9, Crawford
County, Michigan)

Year	Favorable Jack Pine Habitat (ha)	Number of Singing Males Present	Average Size of Territories	
			Considering Available Habitat (ha)	Estimated on Aerial Photograph (ha)
1967–1970	0	0	—	—
1971	0	0	—	—
1972	179	1[1]	unlimited	35.0
1973	179	8	22.4	7.5
1974	179	20	8.95	7.1
1975	179	28	6.39	5.9
1976	179	34	5.26	4.9
1977	195	34	5.73	5.1
1978	195	31	6.3	6.3
1979	195	35	5.57	5.57
1980	195	49	3.98	3.98
1981	195	39	5.0	5.0
Total	1691	278	6.08	5.70

[1]Males observed on area in 1972 not included.

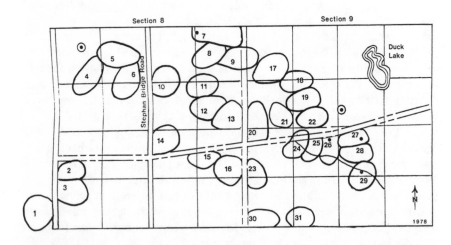

FIGURE 22. Kirtland's Warbler Territories in 1978 on the Artillery Range
North. There had been no warblers on the Artillery Range South after 1977.
Since 1976 there were two to five males on an area about two miles south
of the Artillery Range South which was called the Kyle Lake Shelling Zone.
Ryel (1980) called this area the Artillery Range South.

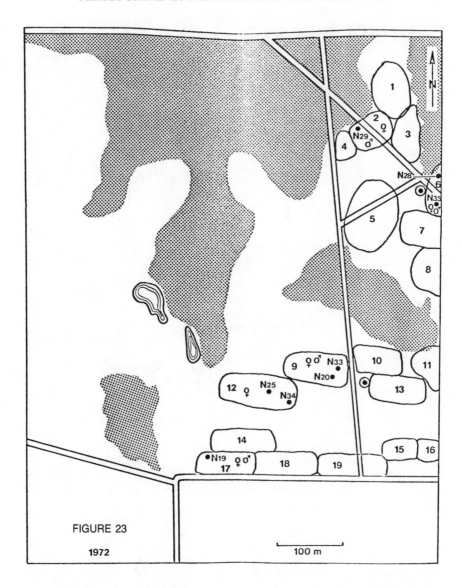

FIGURE 23

1972

100 m

FIGURES 23–29.   Kirtland's Warbler Territories on the Lovells Management Area. These figures show a gradual entry into the 1960 planting (on the southwest side of the road) during the years 1972 through 1978. Stippling indicates mature jack pine forest.

Black circles = Nest locations
Open circle with dot = Active cowbird trap
♂ = Banded male
♀ = Banded female

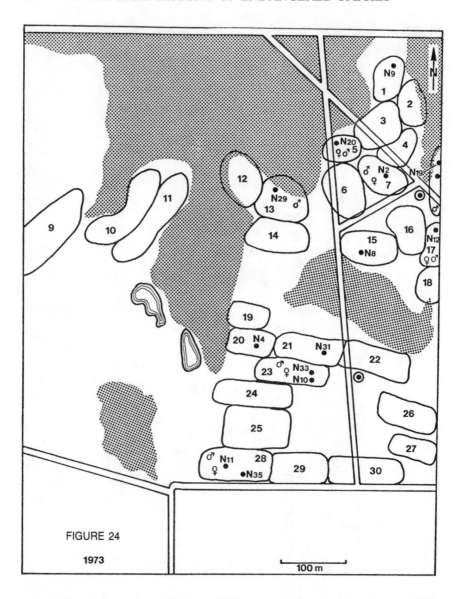

FIGURE 24

1973

100 m

ha. In each of these cases, the small jack pines were surrounded by taller jack pines. In one 24 ha area there was a population of four or five singing males during the period 1976 to 1981. Several nests were found in this region showing that the birds were mated. Nests were not found on other small territories, thus, it is uncertain whether the males located there were mated or not. On the Artillery Range South certain regions were preferred to oth-

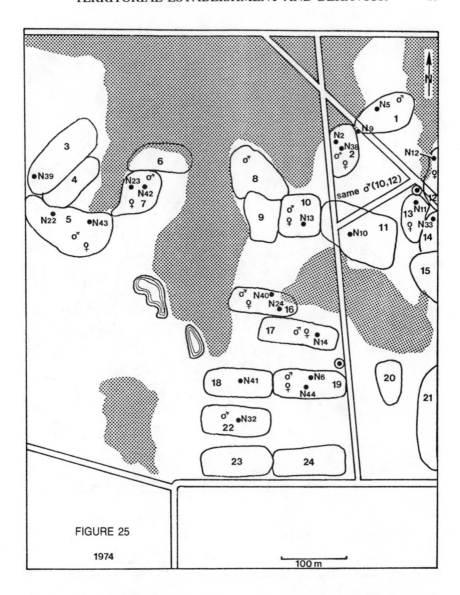

FIGURE 25

1974

100 m

ers. In 1970 a stretch of forest 859 m long contained six nests in use simultaneously. These nests were an average of 172 m apart (range, 98 m to 293 m).

Most territories in natural habitat are roughly circular. Territories in the Lovells Management Area, however, were more rectangular since the trees were planted in rows. The birds avoid the large grassy clearings on each side of the stands and only fly across them occasionally. In section 5 at

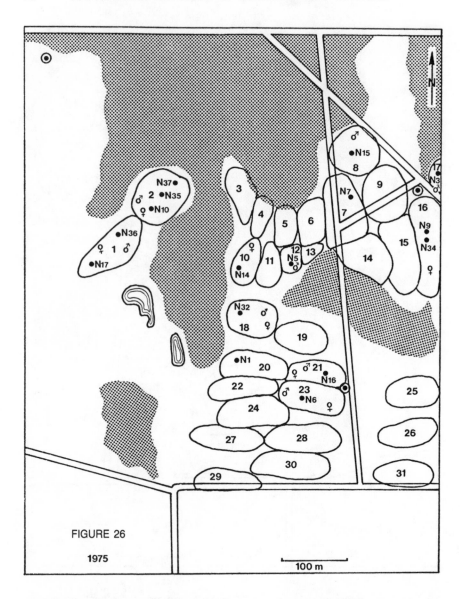

FIGURE 26

1975

100 m

Lovells birds nested regularly from 1971 to 1980, but an area in section 6 which looked equally suitable had few or no nesting warblers. The trees were planted in both regions in 1960. Birds gradually moved into section 5 between 1971 and 1978 and had completely disappeared by 1982 (Figures 24–30). The trees in section 5 (lower right corner of Figure 24) where males 10, 11, 13, 15, and 16 were found in 1972 had been planted in 1958. No

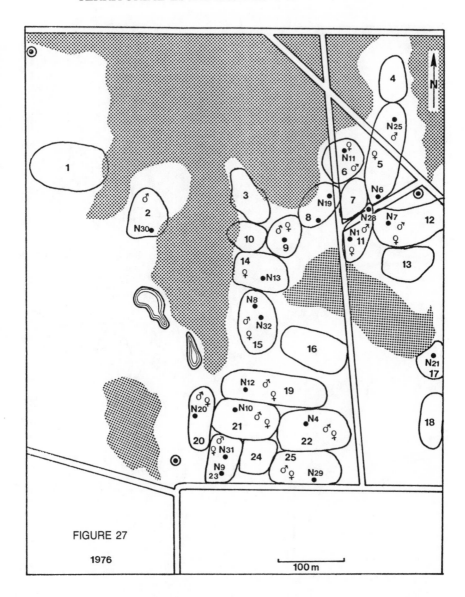

FIGURE 27

1976

100 m

birds were found in this planting after 1977. Only one male was found in all the 1960 plantings during 1982. Thus, these two regions were inhabited for 19 years and 22 years, respectively, after they were planted.

The numbers of singing males recorded by the author from 1972–1982 at Muskrat Lake are given in Table 2. Their distribution through the square

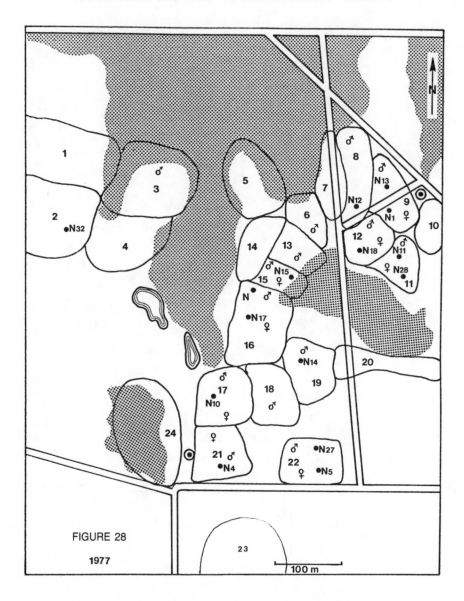

FIGURE 28

1977

100 m

mile section studied was similar to that seen on the Artillery Range. This region burned in 1964 and was still being used extensively in 1982.

Summary

Kirtland's Warblers prefer territories where the jack pines are small. On the Artillery Range North, young males began moving in six years after the

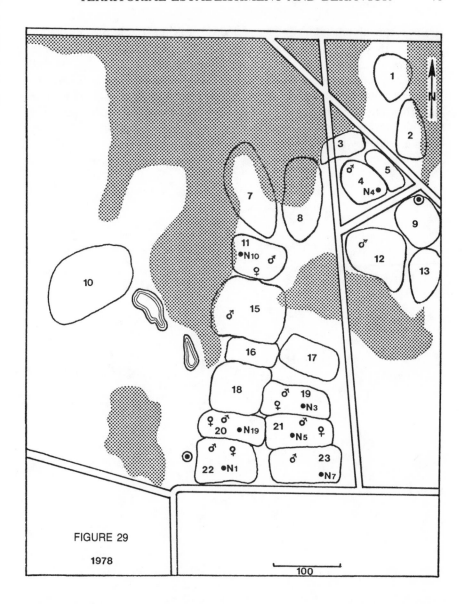

FIGURE 29

1978

area was burned. In this region, the stands in which male warblers bred were statistically younger than the stands in which they were hatched. At the Lovells Management Area five of nine males that hatched returned to the region to breed in subsequent years. As the population in a region increases, the territories decrease in size. When the population decreases, the territories again become larger. Habitat utilization in naturally burned regions reaches a peak 11–17 years following the fire. After this time, the region is quickly abandoned. The period of peak utilization of a plantation came 13–18 years following the planting of the trees. These figures can vary depending upon the growth rate of jack pines in other regions. All regions had been abandoned 22 years following a fire or planting. Kirtland's Warbler territories in summer are extensive, ranging from 4.12 ha to 8.48 ha. When the territory is large much of the border area is not used. The birds seem to favor certain regions over others and the reason for this may be their tendency to form colonies.

CHAPTER 8

NESTING

Mayfield (1960) describes the selection of a nest site and nest-building behavior in detail. The material in this chapter provides additional information on this subject.

Site Selection

Female Kirtland's Warblers arrive at their breeding grounds after 18 May. Under normal conditions, they have selected a mate, built a nest, and laid their first clutch of eggs by 1 June. A female takes only a few hours to select a nest site. She does this by examining the possibilities in her territory. She then makes her selection and begins the construction of the nest. It is unwise to examine the nest site at this time because the female will often desert the site and select a new location.

All of the 339 Kirtland's Warbler nests which I have observed were built in or under ground vegetation approximately 8–20 cm high. Most of the nests were sunken so as to be flush with the ground surface. The nests were usually located in areas where they were shaded by small jack pines and well concealed by lush ground cover. Nests were never found on steep hills, but always on level ground or gentle slopes.

The plants occurring in the vicinity of six Kirtland's Warbler nests were quantitatively analyzed. The procedure used in this analysis placed the nest at the intersection of two perpendicular lines, each 2 m in length. The stems of the plants found in the resulting four-meter-square quadrants were counted. The results of the quantitative analysis are listed in Tables 10 and 11. Approximately 40% of the stems found in these quadrants were blueberry (*Vaccinium angustifolium* and *Vaccinium angustifolium* var. *nigrum*). Wintergreen (*Gaultheria procumbens*) and sweet fern (*Comptonia peregrina*) comprised approximately 20% and 12%, respectively, of the vegetation found in these quadrants. A qualitative description of the vegetation surrounding 283 Kirtland's Warbler nests (Table 12) yields data similar to the small quantitative analysis detailed above. Blueberry and/or grasses comprised the major ground cover around 84.8% of the nests studied.

It has been demonstrated that Kirtland's Warblers nest primarily in regions characterized by small jack pines of uniform height. Such regions are created naturally by forest fires and the birds will utilize a region 5–20 years following a fire. Many stubs often persist in the burned region and mature trees extend along the periphery. The warblers prefer an area containing dense stands of small trees scattered among more widely spaced stands of trees and clearings devoid of trees. The spacing of trees on a naturally burned region can vary from close proximity to 4–5 m apart. The average distance between 500 trees on natural burns used by nesting warblers was 1.0 ± 0.8 m (range, 0.25 m to 6.7 m).

The trees found in warbler habitat usually range in height from 1.2 m to 6.7 m. All the nests included in this study were constructed on the ground in lush vegetation 0–305 cm from the base of the nearest live tree ($\bar{x} = 47.3 \pm 55.7$ cm; $N = 139$). The tree nearest to each nest averaged 2.7 ± 1.3 m in height (range, 0.3 m to 6.4 m; $N = 135$). Out of a total of 146 nests, 139 nests had a jack pine as the closest tree, 2 nests had a quaking aspen as the closest tree, and 5 nests had a small oak as the closest tree. Even when the nest was closest to a tree other than a jack pine, there were small jack pines located very nearby. Up to the present time, Kirtland's Warblers have not been found nesting under natural conditions where jack pines are not the dominant tree. However, the number of male warblers that settled on the Damon burn, Ogemaw County, indicates that they will accept a region with equal numbers of jack pines and oaks.

Nests are often found near or at the edge of a fairly dense growth of jack pines. Out of a group of 126 nests found in naturally burned areas, 22 nests were located exactly on the edge of an opening while 40 nests were located within the pine growth. Sixty-four nests were placed an average of 60 ± 68 cm (range, 1 cm to 366 cm) out from the edge of the trees in an opening.

The Lovells Management Area is an example of a man-made warbler habitat. Here jack pines were planted in groups of 10 rows each with 27 m grassy clearings on either side of each planting. A number of the planted trees had died so there were also additional clearings within the 10-row plantings. One such 10-row planting is represented in Figure 30 which shows the location of all the Kirtland's Warbler nests found in all plantings from 1972 through 1977. This figure demonstrates that the warblers tended to nest on or near the edges of a planting. Out of a total of 79 nests, 40 (50.6%) were located between or very near to the first and second rows of the planting, with 22 of the nests located on the north side of the planting and 18 of the nests located on the south side of the planting. Ten of the total 79 nests (12.7%) were located away from the edges. The remaining 33 nests (41.8%) were located deeper inside the planting, but were often near an area where several trees had died.

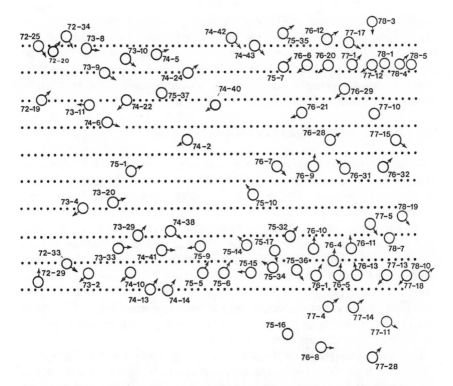

FIGURE 30. Nest Locations on the Lovells Management Area, 1972–1978. The dots indicate rows of trees. The trees were planted 1.2 m apart and the rows were spaced 1.8 m apart. The first two digits refer to the year of the nest and the second two digits refer to the nest number that year.

Nest Construction

A female often begins the construction of a nest by digging a small pit in the sand beneath the vegetation. The nest may be located directly adjacent to a pine or it may be in one of the openings among the groups of pines. Frequently, the nest is located in a position where the female can approach it through fairly dense pine branches 0.6–1.2 m above the ground. The female will seldom approach the nest from higher up or lower down, but remains in this dense stratum. As she nears her nest she briefly drops to the more open level below and moves from branch to branch. Upon arrival at the nest site, she drops onto the ground with the nesting materials. She gathers these materials (dead grasses, leaves, etc.) 2–60 m or more from the nest site. The female first brings coarse materials including large grass culms, small dead leaves, and small pieces of bark or wood to the nest site. She places these in the pit she has dug in the sandy soil. As the materials accumulate, she begins to shape the nest with her body and bill. When the nest reaches her size, she adds finer materials including grasses, sedges, deer hair, moss sporangia, and even fine porcupine quills. The nest site is normally well hidden by vegetation 8–20 cm tall.

Nesting Materials, Weights, and Measurements

Field observations were made on a total of 339 Kirtland's Warbler nests. The grasses most commonly used in these nests were big bluestem grass (*Andropogon gerardii*), little bluestem grass (*Andropogon scoparius*), and oatgrass (*Danthonia spicata*). Sedges (*Carex pensylvanica*) and the leaves of oaks (*Quercus ellipsoidalis*), service-berry (*Amelanchier* sp.), and sand cherry (*Prunus pumila*) were also used as nesting materials. Southern (1961) has performed a detailed botanical analysis of the materials used in the construction of Kirtland's Warbler nests and Mayfield (1960) also discussed the materials used in nest construction. Four nests I examined had 1,464, 1,299, 1,133, and 836 pieces of material, respectively, in them. One of these nests had 431 coarse pieces on the exterior and 868 fine pieces, primarily grasses, on the interior. This nest weighed 2.1 g.

The average weight of 48 dried nests (after use) was 9.4 ± 4.0 g (range, 1.9 g to 18.6 g). The average inside measurement of 54 nests from front to rear was 55.0 ± 6.0 mm (range, 44.0 to 73.0 mm). "Front" refers to the direction from which the nest was entered. The average inside measurement of 47 nests from side to side was 54.0 ± 6.0 mm (range, 44.0 mm to 71.0 mm). The average depth of 52 nests was 38.0 ± 8.0 mm (range, 23.0 mm to 60.0 mm). The exterior measurements of 29 nests averaged 109.0 ± 21.0 mm (range, 81.0 mm to 183.0 mm) from front to rear, 110.0 ± 13.0 mm (range, 81.0 mm to 135.0 mm; N = 28) from side to side, and 48.0 ± 7.0 mm (range 36.0 mm to 58.0 mm; N = 27) in depth.

The front wall or "porch" of the nest was often rather elaborate. The average width of this front "porch" for 13 nests was 45.0 ± 24.0 mm (range, 26.0 mm to 101.0 mm). The side and rear walls of these nests were much thinner, varying between 14 mm and 24 mm in width. The front "porch" of the nest was often located flush with the ground and was usually constructed of fine, well-packed grasses.

Kirtland's Warbler nests occasionally lacked the rough exterior portion and in such cases, they closely resembled the early nest of the Field Sparrow (*Spizella pusilla*). Warbler nests of this type were built slightly above ground level and were well hidden in the dead grasses left from the previous season. When the new season's growth of grasses appeared, these nests became even more effectively camouflaged.

Nearly all Kirtland's Warbler nests have specific entrances, and thus, have a specific directional orientation (Table 17). More of the nests examined in the field faced the south and east (134 each) than faced the west (103) or the north (102). Mayfield (1960) noted a similar tendency in nest orientation; however, this orientation may be due to chance or to a variety of specific conditions at each nest site. Occasionally, a nest was placed beneath a canopy of vegetation and had no distinctive entrance or orientation.

Personal Observations

Most Kirtland's Warblers built their nests on sunny days during the morning (0730 hrs to 1130 hrs EST), but on 24 May 1975 a female was observed building a nest between 1130 hrs EST and dusk. During late May, nest construction was often halted by cold, rainy weather. The first spring nest generally required more time to construct than did the second nest of the season. Eight first nests required three days to build, while two others were finished in two days. Three second nests were completed in two days, while a fourth required three days for completion. Following the completion of the first nest, an average of 2.7 days (range, one day to four days; N = 15) elapsed before the first egg was laid. After the completion of the second nest, one day (twice) and three days (twice) elapsed before the first egg appeared.

A female Kirtland's Warbler was observed while she built her nest south of Lovells, Crawford County, on 31 May 1931. The female and her mate were close together when the female suddenly began gathering fine grasses with her bill. Once she had filled her bill, she disappeared into a dense

TABLE 17. Orientation of Kirtland's Warbler Nests.

Principal Compass Direction	Artillery Range	Lovells Management Area	Other	Total	Percent of Total
North	18	5	3	26	8.9
Northeast	32	15		47	16.1
Northwest	20	9		29	9.9
East	20	7	1	28	9.6
Southeast	43	13	3	59	20.2
South	15	2	1	18	6.2
Southwest	37	19	1	57	19.5
West	12	2	3	17	5.8
No direction (Under canopy)	10	1		11	3.8
Totals	207	73	12	292	100.0

portion of a nearby grove of jack pines. I crawled along the ground in that direction (to approximately 6 m from the nest site) and soon saw her again with another bill full of grass. She seemed agitated and began wagging her tail. Then she disappeared into a thick growth of blueberry and bearberry, emerging one minute later with an empty bill. Since she flew some distance away, I took this opportunity to inspect the nest site. The pit had been dug, but was only partially filled with nesting materials. Every few minutes the female would return with nesting materials and deposit them in the depression. She worked her way back and forth through the jack pines between the nest site and the place where she gathered the nesting materials (a distance of about 60 m). On each of the trips, the female was accompanied by her mate who followed a meter or more behind her, singing as he flew. This pair was first located at 0900 hrs EST and the female was still working on the nest at 1130 hrs EST when the observation was discontinued.

A second female was observed building a nest on the Artillery Range South on 18 June 1972. As the nest neared completion, she became aware of a root extending through the center of the nest. She tugged repeatedly at the root and finally succeeded in removing the outer covering. However, she could not dislodge the root itself and as a result she abandoned this nest site for another.

CHAPTER 9

EGGS

Description

Kirtland's Warbler eggs are ovoid, have a whitish or pinkish ground color, and are covered with varying numbers of brownish spots which are often concentrated in a cap or wreath at the larger end. Some eggs are nearly elliptical in shape with both ends of uniform size. Some have spots distributed over the entire surface. A few eggs have spots concentrated only at the smaller end. The average length of 253 eggs measured in the field (1938–1978) was 18.3 ± 0.7 mm (range, 15.5 mm to 19.9 mm), and the average width (at the widest point) was 14.2 ± 0.6 mm (range, 10.8 mm to 16.0 mm). The average elongation ratio of these eggs (length divided by width) was 1.29 mm.

Forty-five eggs had an average weight of 1.8 g. Weights were determined by weighing the entire clutch at one time. Only abandoned or infertile eggs were measured and no eggs were weighed after 1973 in order to minimize disturbance of nesting birds. This fact introduces a possible source of bias to the data. However, these measurements are very close to those reported

TABLE 18. Number of Kirtland's Warbler Eggs per Nest, 1957–1971.

	No. Eggs Per Nest						Total	Total	Mean Number of Eggs
Year	0	1	2	3	4	5	Nests	Eggs	Observed
1957			2	3	4	2	11	39	3.45
1966	5	1		1			7	4	0.57
1967	2		1	1	2		6	13	2.17
1968				1			1	4	4.00
1969	1	1	2	2	2	1	9	24	2.67
1970		3	1	6	5	1	16	48	3.00
1971	1		9	2		1	13	29	2.23
TOTAL	9	5	15	15	14	5	63	161	2.56

Both parasitized and unparasitized nests are included.

TABLE 19. Sizes of First Clutches, 1972–1978.

Year	No. of Eggs Observed in Nest							Known Completed First Clutches			Eggs in all First Nests		
	0	1	2	3	4	5	6	Total Nests	Total Eggs	Mean Clutch Size	Total Nests with Eggs	Total Eggs	Mean No. of Eggs per Nest
1972													
(I)	4	1	1										
(C)				1	3	19		23	110	4.78	25	113	4.52
1973													
(I)	1	2	1										
(C)					6	20		26	124	4.77	29	128	4.41
1974													
(I)	3	1	2	3	1								
(C)					14	25	1	40	187	4.68	47	205	4.36

TABLE 19. Continued.

Year	No. of Eggs Observed in Nest							Known Completed First Clutches			Eggs in all First Nests		
	0	1	2	3	4	5	6	Total Nests	Total Eggs	Mean Clutch Size	Total Nests with Eggs	Total Eggs	Mean No. of Eggs per Eggs per Nest
1975													
(I)		1	2	1									
(C)				1	7	21		29	136	4.69	33	144	4.36
1976													
(I)		2	3	1									
(C)					3	17		20	97	4.85	26	108	4.15
1977													
(I)			1	1	1								
(C)					4	17		21	101	4.81	24	110	4.58
1978													
(C)					1	8	3	12	62	5.17	12	62	5.17
Total													
(I)	8	7	10	6	2								
(C)				2	38	127	4	171	817	4.78	196	870	4.44

Both parasitized and unparasitized nests are included, but only warbler eggs were counted.
I = incomplete clutches
C = complete clutches

by Mayfield (1960) and this indicates that the amount of bias was probably negligible.

Four eggs in a first clutch laid by a one-year-old female averaged 18.7 mm × 13.9 mm in size. This same female laid eggs the following summer that averaged 19.0 mm × 14.5 mm in size. Another female of unknown age laid an egg in 1969 that measured 17.8 mm × 13.7 mm and a clutch of four eggs in 1970 that averaged 17.7 mm × 14.3 mm. A third female laid a clutch of four eggs in 1969 that averaged 17.1 mm × 14.5 mm and a clutch of five eggs in 1973 that averaged 16.8 mm × 14.0 mm. A fourth female laid a clutch of four eggs in 1970 that averaged 18.1 mm × 14.4 mm. This same female laid a clutch of five eggs in 1971 that averaged 17.8 mm × 14.6 mm.

Clutch Size

Between 1931 and 1955, I observed 17 nests of Kirtland's Warbler with completed first clutches (eggs laid in late May or early June). These nests contained 85 warbler eggs and no cowbird eggs or an average of 5 warbler eggs per clutch. One known second clutch contained four eggs. During the period of most active cowbird parasitism (1957–1971), 16 of 63 warbler nests were unparasitized, but five of these contained only two eggs or nestlings indicating their clutches were incomplete. The other 11 unparasitized first clutches contained 41 warbler eggs or 3.73 eggs per clutch (Table 18).

During the period when adult Brown-headed Cowbirds were removed from warbler regions (1972–1978), 817 eggs were found in 171 nests or an average of 4.78 eggs per clutch (Table 19). Thirty-six second unparasitized clutches from the years 1972 through 1977 had an average clutch size of four eggs (Table 20). A decrease in clutch size was recorded as the summer advanced (Table 21). Most unparasitized first clutches had five eggs, while most unparasitized second clutches had four eggs. The data show that clutch size was definitely affected by cowbird parasitism. Even when eggs were not removed or nests parasitized, the clutch size was smaller in unparasitized first clutches during the years of active cowbird parasitism (1957–1971) (Tables 22, 23, and 24).

During the years 1931 through 1955, the average clutch size was five eggs, but the average clutch size declined to 3.73 eggs during the years 1957 through 1971 when cowbird parasitism was most severe. The average clutch size increased to 4.78 eggs during the years 1972 through 1978, after cowbird removal was instituted. None of the nests utilized to derive these figures was parasitized. The size of observed clutches (after cowbirds had removed all or part of the original clutch) in parasitized nests was two eggs (range, 0–5 KW eggs). One nest held five warbler eggs and two cowbird eggs, while another held four warbler eggs and three cowbird eggs. During the

TABLE 20. Sizes of Unparasitized First and Second Clutches.

Year	1st Clutch 3	4	5	6	Total Nests	Total Eggs	Mean Clutch	2nd Clutch 3	4	5	Total Nests	Total Eggs	Mean Clutch Size	Both Clutches 3	4	5	6	Total Nests	Total Eggs	Mean Clutch Size
1972	1	3	19		23	110	4.78	2	4		6	22	3.67	3	7	19		29	132	4.55
1973		6	20		26	124	4.77	1	1	3	5	22	4.40	1	7	23		31	146	4.71
1974		14	25	1	40	187	4.68	1	5	3	9	38	4.22	1	19	28	1	49	225	4.59
1975	1	7	21		29	136	4.69		2	2	4	18	4.50	1	9	23		33	154	4.67
1976		3	17		20	97	4.85	1	5		6	23	3.83	1	8	17		26	120	4.62
1977		4	17		21	101	4.81	3	3		6	21	3.50	3	7	17		27	122	4.52
1978	1	1	8	3	12	62	5.17	—	—	—	—	—	—	—	—	—	—	—	—	—
Totals	2	38	127	4	171	817	4.78	8	20	8	36	144	4.00	10	57	127	1	195	899	4.61
														10	58	135	4	207	961	4.64

TABLE 21.   Clutch Sizes By Month Excluding 14 Parasitized Nests, 1972–1977.

Month	May				June			July					
Clutch Size Year	3	4	5	6	3	4	5	3	4	5	Total Nests	Total Eggs	Mean Clutch Size
1972		2	8		1	2	11	1	3		28	129	4.61
1973			6			6	17	1	1		31	146	4.71
1974		4	15	1		12	12	1	2	2	49	226	4.61
1975	1	4	17			5	5			1	33	154	4.67
1976		2	14		1	5	3		1		26	120	4.62
1977		2	14		2	5	3	1			27	122	4.52
Total Nests	1	14	74	1	4	35	51	4	7	3	194		
Total Eggs	3	56	370	6	12	140	255	12	28	15		897	
Mean Clutch Size		4.83				4.52			3.93				4.62

TABLE 22.   Clutch Size in Parasitized Nests vs. Unparasitized Nests, 1931–1955.

	Unparasitized Nests			Parasitized Nests					
KW Eggs in Unpara- sitized Nests	Total Nests	Total Eggs in Unpara- sitized Nests	Cowbird Eggs 1	 2	 3	Total C Eggs	Total KW Nests Para- sitized	Total KW Eggs in Para- sitized
0			1		1	4	2	0
1				1		2	1	1
2				1		2	1	2
3				1		2	1	3
4	2	8	2			2	2	
5	15	75						
6	1	6						
Totals	18	89	3	3	1	12	7	14
Average Clutch Size		4.94 KW				1.71 C		2.0 KW

KW = Kirtland's Warbler
C = Cowbird

TABLE 23. Clutch Size in Parasitized Nests vs. Unparasitized Nests, 1957–1971.

Unparasitized Nests			Parasitized Nests						
No. of KW Eggs per Nest	No. of Nests	Total KW Eggs in Unparasitized Nests	No. of Cowbird Eggs					No. of KW Nests	Total No. KW Eggs in Parasitized Nests
			1	2	3	4	Total		
0	(5)	0	5	3		1	15	9	0
1			1	3		1	10	5	5
2	4	8	6	3	2		18	11	22
3	6	18	4	5			14	9	27
4	4	16	8	1		1	13	10	40
5	2	10	2	1			4	3	15
Total	16	52	26	16	4	1	74	47	109
Total C Eggs			26	32	12	4			
Average Clutch Size		3.25					1.57		2.32

The average clutch size for all nests was 2.56 KW eggs per clutch.

years 1931–1955, seven parasitized nests held 12 cowbird eggs (1.7 cowbird eggs per parasitized nest). Forty-seven of 63 nests observed from 1957 to 1971 were parasitized (74.6%), indicating a much higher level of parasitism than was observed during the years 1931 to 1955. The average number of cowbird eggs per nest (1957–1971) was 1.6 eggs (Table 23). During the years 1972 through 1978, 14 nests were parasitized. These nests contained 24 warbler eggs and 21 cowbird eggs. One nest contained five warbler eggs and one cowbird egg. Another nest held five warbler eggs and two cowbird eggs, indicating that the cowbird did not remove any warbler eggs. Both nests were watched until termination and they never lost warbler eggs in the usual manner. On seven occasions, warbler nests held one cowbird egg; on four occasions, two cowbird eggs; on one occasion, three cowbird eggs; and on another occasion, four cowbird eggs. On ten occasions, warbler nests held a number of cowbird eggs but only one warbler egg (Table 25).

Eleven one-year-old females laid an average of 4.82 ± 0.40 eggs (range, four eggs to five eggs) in their first year (Table 26). Table 26 shows the clutch sizes of several females for more than one year. These data indicate that clutch size is not dependent upon the female's age.

TABLE 24.   Clutch Size in Parasitized Nests vs. Unparasitized Nests, 1972–1978.

	Unparasitized Nests		Parasitized Nests				
No. of KW Eggs in Nest	No. of Nests	Total KW Eggs in Unparasitized Nests	No. of Cowbird Eggs			No. of KW Nests	Total No. of KW Eggs in Parasitized Nests
			1	2	Total		
0	(10)*	0	1	1	3	2	0
1	5	5	1	3	7	4	4
2	6	12	2	3	8	5	10
3	17	51	2		2	2	6
4	59	236	1		1	1	4
5	135	675					
6	4	24					
Total	226	1,003	7	7	21	14	24
Average Clutch Size		4.44			1.50		1.71

*10 warbler nests were observed with neither warbler or cowbird eggs. These nests are not included in the totals.
Nineteen nests (5 × 1; 6 × 2, 7 × 3, 1 × 4 eggs) did not have completed clutches.

Laying of First Eggs in Spring

With the exception of three one-year-old females who first nested in late June, 152 females laid their first eggs in the spring between 21 May (1976) and 12 June (1974). The average date was 31 May. These dates are only a rough estimate since the number of days spent in the field each year varied and early nests during 1970 and 1971 could have been missed. Nevertheless, it is evident that females laid their first eggs during the last week in May or the first ten days in June. A summary of these data as well as data concerning hatching and fledging of young is shown in Tables 27 and 28.

Thirteen one-year-old females laid their first eggs between 28 May and 27 June (Table 29). Seven of these females laid their first eggs when they were two years old between 24 May and 5 June ($\bar{x}$ = 30 May), while three of these females laid their first eggs when they were three years old between 28 May and 30 May ($\bar{x}$ = 29 May). Two females, when five years old, laid their first eggs on 27 and 28 May, respectively. One seven-year-old female laid her first egg on 11 June. The average age of females when they laid their first eggs was 354.2 ± 14.7 days.

Warren Faust and I studied one female Kirtland's Warbler during six summers (she was not found in 1971) (Walkinshaw 1977). She laid her first

TABLE 25. Clutch Sizes in Parasitized Nests vs. Unparasitized Nests, Summary 1931–1977.

	Unparasitized Nests					Parasitized Nests			
Years	No. of Nests	Total KW Eggs	x̄ KW Eggs Nest	Total Nests and Percent		No. of KW Eggs	No. of KW Eggs per Nest	Total C Eggs	C Eggs per Parasitized Nest
1931–1955	18	89	4.9	7	28.0%	14	2.0	12	1.7
1957–1971	16	52	3.3	47	74.6%	109	2.3	74	1.6
1972–1978	207	961	4.6	14	6.3%	24	1.7	21	1.5
Total	241	1,102	4.6	68	22.0%	147	2.2	107	1.6

TABLE 26.   Clutch Size by Age of Female. (All females were banded as nestlings)

No.	Band Number	Age: N =	Clutch sizes for females of known age during different breeding seasons							Years
			1 13	2 8	3 4	4 0	5 2	6 0	7 2	
1.	110-09079							5	5	
2.	116-24635			5					4	
3.	850-72516		5							
4.	81-58948		5				5			
5.	81-58914			3, 5	5, 5					
6.	81-58968		1+							
7.	81-58978		4	5, 1+						
8.	820-89228		5							
9.	820-89229				5, 5					
10.	820-89252			5, 5						
11.	820-89269		5							
12.	820-89288		4	4						
13.	830-20517		5	5, 3	5					
14.	830-20530		5, 4	5	4					
15.	830-20532		4+							
16.	830-20555			5, 4						
17.	860-40330		5							
18.	860-40326		5, 4							
19.	860-40343		5, 4							
Mean Clutch Size	First Clutch		4.82	4.62	4.75	5.00	4.50			
	Second Clutch		4.00	4.25	5.00					

+ = Actual clutch size was unknown. These figures were not included in the computation of mean clutch size.

eggs on the following dates (some dates were calculated from the known time of hatching and fledging): 4–7 June 1970, late May 1972, 2–5 July 1972 (second clutch), 2–5 June 1973, 3–5 July 1973 (second clutch), 27–31 May 1974, 3–6 July 1974 (second clutch), 28 May–1 June 1975, 30 May–3 June 1976.

The onset of laying of first clutches was affected by air temperature. When the temperature exceeded 20°C for a prolonged period of time egg-laying could start as early as 23 May (Figures 31 and 32). However, in 1976 two females laid their first eggs on 21 May and 23 May even though the preceding weather was not extremely warm (the average temperature had not exceeded 15.6°C). Apparently, a higher average temperature had more in-

TABLE 27. Date of First Egg-Laying.

Year	May 21	22	23	24	25	26	27	28	29	30	31	June 1	2	3	4	5	6	7	8	9	10	11	12	Total
1970											2	1	1	1	2									7
1971											1	1	1	3		1	1							8
1972			1			2	1	2	4	1		1	5				1							18
1973								1	1		4		1	2	1	4	1			1				16
1974			2		1		3	4	2	1	1	1	3	1	3	1		2				1		26
1975					4	2	3	3	4	7	2			4		1						2		32
1976	2			1	1	1	2	3	4	2		3					1		1	1		1		23
1977			1	2	1		6	5		2						2				1			2	22
Totals	2		4	3	7	5	15	18	15	13	10	7	11	11	6	9	4	2	1	3		4	2	152

Mean date: 31 May

Numbers of females laying eggs on any given date are listed in the Table and in Figures 31 and 32.

Some of these dates were estimated from the date of hatching (allowing 14 days for incubation).

TABLE 28.   Earliest, Latest, and Peak Periods of Eggs and Nestlings.

Year	Date First Egg was Laid	Peak Period for Eggs in all Nests	Date First Egg Hatched	Date Last Egg Hatched	Peak Period for Nestlings in all Nests	Date Last Nestling Fledged
1972	5/23	6/8	6/9	7/23	6/20	8/1
1973	5/28	6/13	6/14	7/22	6/24–6/27	7/31
1974	5/23	6/10	6/11	7/22	6/21	8/1
1975	5/25	6/7	6/10	7/18	6/20–6/22	7/29
1976	5/21	6/6	6/7	7/19	6/18	7/25
1977	5/23	6/7	6/8	7/20	6/18	7/29
Mean	5/24	6/8	6/10	7/21	6/20–6/21	7/29

fluence on egg-laying than did occasional frosty nights. Other factors such as food supply and nesting cover also effect the onset of egg-laying. Table 30 demonstrates that the temperature 5–6 days prior to egg-laying averaged 2°C warmer than the temperature on the day when the first egg was actually laid.

Average egg-laying dates for first and second clutches from 1970 through 1977 are listed in Table 31. Extreme dates are also given. The average period when the first clutch of five eggs was laid was 30 May–3 June. The average date of hatching was 16–17 June and the average date of fledging was 26 June. The average period when the second clutch of four eggs was laid was 28 June–1 July. The average date of hatching was 14–15 July and the average date of fledging was 24 July.

For the years 1972 through 1977, the average dates when maximum numbers of eggs were present in Kirtland's Warbler nests varied between 6–13 June, with an overall average date of 8–9 June (Figures 33 and 34; Table 28). Average dates of maximum nestling abundance varied between 18–27 June, with an overall average date of 20–21 June. In part these averages reflect the dates when the first egg was laid, the first egg hatched, and the last egg hatched (Table 28). Dates when the last nestling fledged varied over an eight day period from 25 July to 1 August (Figures 33 and 34).

Incubation

Female Kirtland's Warblers lay one egg per day, usually during the early morning, until the clutch is complete. Incubation was normally performed only by the female and began the afternoon before the last egg was laid.

TABLE 29. First Nestings of One-Year-Old Females.

No.	Band Number	Date Hatched	Dates When First Clutch Was Laid	Age in Days When First Egg Was Laid	Nesting Success		
					Eggs Laid	Hatched	Fledged
5.	81-58948	6/15/72	3–7 June 1973	353	5	5	5
7.	81-58968	6/15/72	–25 June 1973	375	1+	1	1
8.	81-58978	6/16/72	17–20 June 1973	366	4	2	2
9.	820-89228	6/20/73	30 May–3 June 1974	344	5	5	5
12.	820-89269	6/30/73	2–6 June 1974	338	5	4	4
13.	820-89288	7/18/73	7–10 June 1974	324	4	4	4
4.	850-72516	6/13/74	3–7 June 1975	355	5	5	5
14.	830-20517	6/14/74	3–7 June 1975	354	5	4	4
15.	830-20530	6/12/74	31 May–4 June 1975	352	5	0	0
16.	830-20532	6/12/74	27–30 June 1975	380	4	4	4
18.	860-40330	6/12/75	8–12 June 1976	361	5	5	5
19.	860-40326	6/09/76	28 May–1 June 1977	353	5	0	0
20.	860-40343	6/16/76	1–5 June 1977	350	4	2	2
Average		18 June	7 June	354	70	45	45

0.643% of eggs hatched

+ = at least this number of eggs were laid

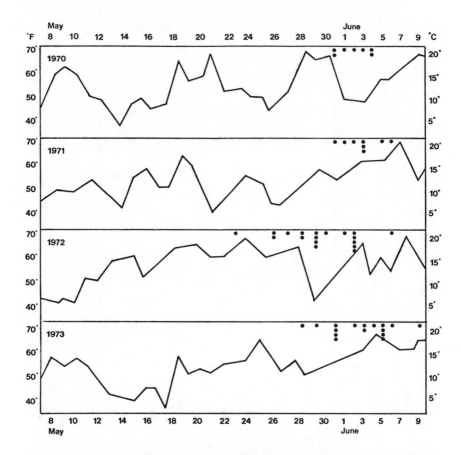

FIGURE 31.   Relationship Between Temperature and Dates When First Eggs Were Laid, 1970–1973. At some nests the laying of the first egg was calculated from the date of hatching, allowing 14 days for incubation. Solid lines connect mean daily temperatures recorded at Grayling, Crawford County, Michigan. Dots indicate dates when first eggs were laid.

Occasionally, a female was found on a nest prior to this time, but only for a short period. Even on nights of heavy frost, females were rarely found on the nest if they were laying. This could account for the fact that eggs in early nests sometimes fail to hatch.

Some males regularly brought food to their mate on the nest, while others seldom, if ever, did. On 1 June 1957 I watched a pair of Kirtland's Warblers at their nest (this was the day on which the last egg was laid). Between 1458 hrs EST and 2020 hrs EST, the female spent 259 minutes of a possible 322 minutes (80.4%) incubating the eggs. She left the nest seven times, each trip averaging seven minutes in length (range, 5 min to 13 min). Time spent

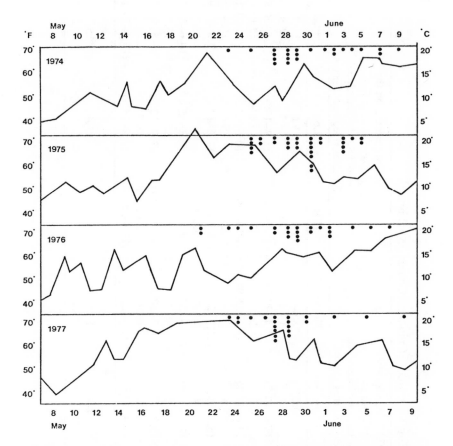

FIGURE 32.   Relationship Between Temperature and Dates When First Eggs
Were Laid, 1974–1977. Data structure similar to that in Figure 31.

on the nest between these absences averaged 37 minutes (range, 20 min to
56 min). The temperature was about 20°C. There was little wind and the
sun set at 2004 hrs EST after which it became much cooler.

Kirtland's Warbler eggs require a relatively long incubation period for a
warbler species. At 21 nests, where 76 of 94 warbler eggs hatched, the
average incubation period was 14.2 days (range, 13 days to 15 days) or 341
hours (range, 312 hours to 360 hours). The incubation period was measured
as the time between the laying and hatching of the last egg. In many nests
it was not possible to determine the exact incubation period because the last
egg failed to hatch. However, the following records were obtained. In 1944
at Nest 1, five eggs were laid on 2–6 June. I did not know the exact time
the fifth egg was laid but the eggs are always laid during the early morning.
On 19 June at 0600 hrs EST there were still five intact eggs in the nest,
although several were pipped considerably. At 0700 hrs EST there were

TABLE 30. Air Temperature When First Egg Was Laid. (Crawford County, Michigan)

Year	Number of Records	Air Temperature 5–6 Days Prior to Laying of First Eggs by Individual Females (Degrees Celsius)			Temperature on the Day the First Egg was Laid by Individual Females (Degrees Celsius)		
		High	Low	Mean	High	Low	Mean
1969	1	32.6	20.0	26.4	17.8	5.6	11.7
1970	8	21.7	9.1	15.4	20.3	9.3	14.8
		(11.5–30.4)	(3.3–17.2)	(7.4–20.7)	(11.7–24.4)	(1.7–18.9)	(7.5–20.8)
1971	9	23.5	4.6	14.1	24.5	9.6	17.0
		(16.1–29.9)	(0.0–12.1)	(8.0–21.0)	(18.9–30.0)	(0.6–12.2)	(11.1–21.1)
1972	19	28.4	5.8	17.1	26.4	5.6	16.0
		(20.0–32.8)	(3.3–10.0)	(11.7–21.3)	(13.3–30.6)	(2.2–10.0)	(7.8–18.9)
1973	11	22.6	5.4	14.0	20.8	9.3	15.1
		(18.3–25.0)	(1.7–19.4)	(10.5–20.2)	(14.4–27.8)	(2.8–15.6)	(10.6–21.7)
1974	27	22.9	10.6	16.7	21.5	5.5	13.5
		(10.5–30.5)	(0.0–12.2)	(6.7–20.2)	(11.7–29.4)	(0.0–12.2)	(8.3–20.3)
1975	23	27.7	11.2	19.7	24.7	8.7	16.7
		(22.2–33.3)	(4.4–17.8)	(15.3–25.5)	(19.4–29.4)	(3.3–15.6)	(13.1–21.1)
7-year Average	98	25.2	7.4	16.3	23.2	7.4	15.3
Extremes		(10.5–33.3)	(0.0–20.0)	(6.7–26.4)	(11.7–30.6)	(0.0–18.9)	(7.5–21.7)

three nestlings and at 1700 hrs EST there were five nestlings. In this case, incubation required about 320 hours and all the eggs hatched during a 10 hour period. In 1974 at Nest 18, the fifth egg was laid on 13 June. The first eggs hatched on 25 June and the last egg hatched on 26 June, 13 days after it was laid. At four other nests the incubation period was apparently 13 days, although not all the eggs hatched.

At seven other nests the eggs hatched in 14 days. For example, in 1972 at Nest 4, the last of five eggs was laid on 6 June. On 19 June at 0500 hrs EST there were still five eggs, but on 20 June at 0800 hrs EST there were five nestlings. Incubation required slightly less than 14 days or 330–335 hours. In 1973 at Nest 7, the fifth egg was laid on 17 June in early morning. On 29 June the nest still contained five eggs. On 30 June at 1300 hrs EST there were four nestlings and one egg. On 1 July at 1000 hrs EST there were five nestlings. In 1974 at Nest 1, the first egg was laid on 2 June and the fifth egg was laid before 1000 hrs EST on 6 June. The female had begun incubating on the afternoon of 5 June. On 19 June four eggs hatched and on 20 June the fifth egg hatched by midday. Incubation required 14 days or 330–335 hours. Also in 1974 at Nest 2, five eggs were laid between 28 May and 1 June. The fifth egg hatched on 15 June, 14 days after it was laid.

At least six nests required an incubation period of 15 days. In 1974 at two nests located within 200 m of each other (Nests 11 and 12), four eggs were laid on the same days (12–15 June). At Nest 11 on 30 June, one egg had disappeared, but at 1300 hrs EST there were three eggs present. At 1500 hrs EST there were three nestlings. They had hatched at least 15 days after the fourth egg was laid. At Nest 12 on 29 June, there were four eggs present at 1400 hrs EST. On 30 June there were three nestlings at 0900 hrs EST. The fourth egg failed to hatch. Thus, the eggs in Nest 12 hatched approximately six hours sooner than the eggs in Nest 11. Also in 1974 at Nest 14, the fourth egg was laid on 10 June and hatched on 25 June.

The nesting grounds were under observation regularly from 1972–1978, and thus, it was possible to obtain the earliest and latest hatching dates for many nests. These data are given in Table 31. The earliest dates for the hatching of first clutches are as follows: 9 June 1972, 14 June 1973, 10 June 1974, 10 June 1975, 7 June 1976, 9 June 1977. The earliest dates for the hatching of second clutches are as follows: 10 July 1972, 5 July 1973, 2 July 1974, 1 July 1975, 30 June 1976, 4 July 1977 (first nests had been destroyed).

Second Nestings

Table 32 summarizes the data relating to 11 pairs of Kirtland's Warblers that nested twice in one summer. Another pair also renested after a suc-

TABLE 31. Average Egg-laying, Hatching, and Fledging Dates (Crawford County and Oscoda County, Michigan). (Kirtland's Warbler eggs and nestlings only).

Year	Average Date Eggs Were Laid	No. of Clutch	No. of Nests	Eggs	Average Date Eggs Hatched	No. of Nests	Average Date Nestlings Fledged	No. of Nests	Young
1970	6/1–6/4	1	8		6/17–6/18	7	6/26	7	
1971	6/4–6/7	1	10		6/19–6/20	7	6/27	6	
1972	5/30–6/3	1	20	87	6/15–6/16 (6/9–7/5)	20	6/25 (6/19–7/15)	17	70
1972	6/30–7/3	2	5	17	7/18 (7/10–7/23)	5	7/28 (7/20–8/1)	5	17
1973	6/3–6/7	1	27	95	6/20–6/21 (6/14–7/3)	23	6/30 (6/25–7/13)	19	77
1973	6/27–6/30	2	5	17	7/13 (7/5–7/19)	5	7/22 (7/15–7/28)	5	13

TABLE 31. Continued

Year	Average Date Eggs Were Laid	No. of Clutch	No. of Nests	Eggs	Average Date Eggs Hatched	No. of Nests	Average Date Nestlings Fledged	No. of Nests	Young
1974	5/31–6/4	1	41	159	6/17–6/18 (6/10–6/30)	40	6/27 (6/21–7/10)	37	143
1974	6/28–7/2	2	11	34	7/15–7/16 (7/2–7/23)	11	7/25 (7/12–8/1)	10	32
1975	5/29–6/2	1	28	102	6/16–6/17 (6/10–6/21)	27	6/26 (6/21–7/8)	22	86
1975	6/25–6/29	2	4	17	7/12 (7/1–7/19)	4	7/22 (7/11–7/29)	4	17
1976	5/29–6/2	1	22	83	6/15–6/16 (6/7–7/3)	21	6/24 (6/17–7/13)	18	73
1976	6/27–6/30	2	6	18	7/13–7/14 (6/30–7/20)	6	7/22 (7/9–7/25)	4	13
1977	5/28–6/1	1	20	74	6/12–6/13 (6/9–7/1)	18	6/23 (6/18–7/11)	15	55
1977	6/27–6/29	2	6	13	7/13–7/14 (7/4–7/20)	5	7/26 (7/10–7/29)	4	9

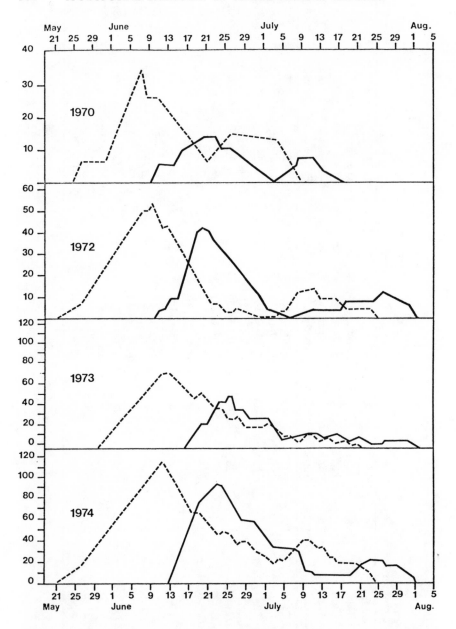

FIGURE 33.   Dates When Eggs (dashed lines) and Nestlings (solid lines) Were Found, 1970–1974. The number of nests studied was not necessarily an index of the number of warblers present. When nests were discovered with nestlings, the dates of hatching and laying were calculated.

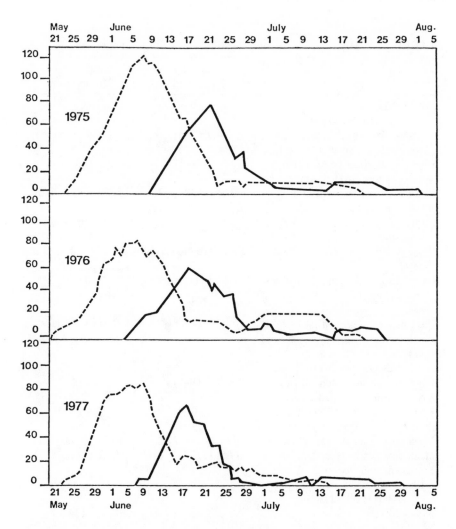

FIGURE 34.   Dates When Eggs (dashed lines) and Nestlings (solid lines)
Were Found 1975–1977. Data structure similar to that in Figure 33.

cessful first nest, but neither of their nest sites were located. This pair was
observed feeding fledged nestlings from an unlocated first nest when they
had eggs in their second nest. The average date when nestlings fledged from
the first nestings of these 11 pairs was 26 June, but on two occasions young
fledged from these 11 nests as late as 1 July. The length of time between
the fledging of nestlings from the first nest and the laying of the first egg
in the second nest averaged 7.1 days (range, 4 days to 11 days).

TABLE 32.   Histories of Second Nestings in a Single Year.

	First Nest Successful	First Nest Unsuccessful
No. of Pairs	11	14
FIRST NESTING		
$\bar{x}$ Size of first clutch (range)	4.7 (3–6)	4.8 (3–5)
$\bar{x}$ No. nestlings hatched (range)	4.5 (3–5)	1.5
$\bar{x}$ No. of nestlings fledged (range)	4.5 (3–5)	0
% of eggs that fledged young	94	0
Mean date first egg was laid	5/29 (5/27–6/3)	5/29 (5/26–6/6)
Mean date nestlings fledged	6/26 (6/22–7/1)	—
Mean date predator removed eggs or nestlings	—	6/18 (6/7–7/1)
Distance between first & second nests	72.4 m (16–137.5 m)	115 m (31.1–323 m)
Days between fledging at first nest and laying of first egg at second nest	7.1 (4–11) days	—
Days between loss of first nest and laying of first egg at second nest	—	6.0 (4–9) days
SECOND NESTING		
$\bar{x}$ Size of second clutch (range)	4.0 (1–5)	4.2 (2–5)
$\bar{x}$ No. nestlings hatched (range)	3.6	2.7
$\bar{x}$ No. of nestlings fledged (range)	3.0 (0–4)	2.4 (0–4)
% of eggs that fledged young	83	60
Mean date first egg was laid	7/3 (6/29–7/6)	6/25 (6/11–7/1)
Mean date nestlings fledged or predator removed eggs or nestlings	7/28 (7/25–8/2)	7/21 (7/12–8/1)
BOTH NESTINGS		
Eggs laid	93	124
Nestlings fledged	83	34
% of eggs from which nestlings fledged	89.2	27.4
$\bar{x}$ No. of nestlings fledged per pair in one breeding season (range)	7.5 (5–9)	2.4 (0–4)
Total no. nestlings returning in later years to study areas (from first nests)	13	0
No. of nestlings returning in later years to study areas from second nests	1	0

Fourteen pairs of warblers lost their first clutch or brood of the year (10 pairs lost eggs, while the remaining four pairs lost nestlings to predators). The elapsed time between the loss of eggs or nestlings and the laying of the first egg in their second nest averaged 6 days (range, 4 days to 9 days). These pairs located their second nest farther away from their first nest than did pairs which achieved a successful first nesting. The average distance between first and second nests was 115 m (range, 31.1 m to 323 m) for the unsuccessful group as compared with 72.4 m (range, 16 m to 137.5 m) for the successful group. No female was found to have more than two clutches of eggs during a single summer. Twenty-five females were known to lay two clutches of eggs. Eleven of these females had successful first broods, while 14 lost either eggs or nestlings to predators and subsequently renested. Of these 25 females, 16 (62%) laid 9–11 eggs, 11 laid 9 eggs, 4 laid 10 eggs, and 1 laid 11 eggs (Table 32).

Summary

If undisturbed by cowbirds, female Kirtland's Warblers will normally lay five eggs in their first clutch. They lay one egg per day until the clutch is complete. The eggs are laid in the early morning often before 0730 hrs EST. The eggs are whitish with brown spots and measure 18.3 ± 0.7 mm (range, 15.5 mm to 19.9 mm) by 14.2 ± 0.6 mm (range, 10.8 mm to 16.0 mm). Each egg weighs about 1.8 g. If a first clutch is lost to a predator, the female will produce a second clutch of four eggs. About half of the older females studied attempted a second nesting after a successful first nesting and produced four eggs in that second clutch. No first year female produced a second clutch in one summer unless the first was destroyed by a predator. Most one-year-old females began laying slightly later in the spring than did older birds, usually between 28 May and 27 June ($\bar{x} = 7$ June). Their average age when the first egg appeared was 354 days (range, 324 days to 380 days). For all nests the earliest date of laying averaged 24 May (range, 21 May to 28 May). Egg-laying was definitely stimulated by warmer temperatures five to six days before the laying of the first egg. The average date of laying for the entire clutch ranged from 28 May to 1 June (1977) to 3 June to 7 June (1973), while hatching occurred between 7 June and 21 June.

Clutches varied from three to six eggs. The field data gathered on 171 clutches of known size showed the following distribution: First clutches— 2 had three eggs, 38 had four eggs, 127 had five eggs, and 4 had six eggs ($\bar{x} = 4.78$ eggs); Second clutches—8 had three eggs, 20 had four eggs, and 8 had five eggs ($\bar{x} = 4.0$ eggs). When first eggs were laid in late May, the average clutch size was 4.83 eggs. The average clutch size of eggs laid in June was 4.52 eggs and the average clutch size of eggs laid in early July was 3.93 eggs. The average clutch size for first nestings for various age groups of females was as follows: one-year-old females—4.82 eggs (N = 12); two-year-old females—4.62 eggs (N = 8); three-year-old females— 4.75 eggs (N = 4); five-year-old females—5.00 eggs (N = 2); seven-year-old females—4.5 eggs (N = 2). Average clutch size for the period prior to severe cowbird parasitism (1931–1955) was 4.94 eggs per unparasitized nest (N = 18). Average clutch size fell to 3.25 eggs per unparasitized nest during the period of severe cowbird parasitism (1957–1971). After the removal of adult cowbirds from major warbler nesting regions (1972–present), clutch size rebounded to 4.44 eggs per nest (N = 226).

Eleven pairs of warblers are known to have attempted a second nesting after a successful first nesting. For these, the average clutch size of the first nesting was 4.7 eggs (range, three eggs to six eggs). The first egg was laid on 29 May (range, 27 May to 3 June) and the nestlings fledged on 26 June (range, 22 June to 1 July). The second nest was located an average distance of 72.4 m (range, 16 m to 137.5 m) from the first nest and the first egg was laid in the second nest an average of 7.1 day (range, 4 days to 11 days) after the young fledged from the first nest. The average clutch size in the second nest was 4.0 eggs (range, one egg to five eggs). The average date of laying the first egg in the second nest was 3 July (range, 29 June to 6 July) and the average date on which young fledged was 28 July (range, 25 July to 2 August).

Fourteen pairs of warblers are known to have lost a first nest to predators during June. For these, the average size of their first clutches was 4.8 eggs (range, three eggs to five eggs). The date of laying of their first eggs ranged between 26 May and 6 June ($\bar{x}$ = 29 May). A predator removed the eggs or nestlings from these nests between 7 June and 1 July ($\bar{x}$ = 18 June). These pairs moved their second nest farther from their first nests than did pairs whose first nest was successful. These females laid the first egg in their second clutch an average of six days after their first nest was destroyed (range, four days to nine days). The average clutch size of the second nesting was 4.2 eggs (range, two eggs to five eggs) of which 2.7 hatched and 2.4 fledged (range, 0–4). The average date of fledging was 21 July (range, 12 July to 1 August). Pairs with successful first nests raised an average of 7.5 fledged nestlings (range, five nestlings to nine nestlings), while pairs that lost their first nest raised only 2.4 fledged nestlings (range, zero nestlings to four nestlings). The pairs which were most successful in their first nestings were also more successful in their second nestings. This may be attributed to behavior, suitability of territory, better selection of nest site, or other reasons.

CHAPTER 10

THE NESTLINGS

Description

When Kirtland's Warblers hatch, they are completely helpless and depend upon their parents for protection, food, and warmth. After hatching, the nestlings initially remain curled up in the bottom of the nest in the fetal position. A description of the prenatal down of Kirtland's Warblers has been recorded by Wetherbee for two individuals (Mayfield 1960). This down is dark brown in contrast to the very light gray or whitish down of cowbird nestlings. At the time of hatching, the Kirtland's Warbler nestling is much smaller than the cowbird nestling. Records of weights and measurements of Kirtland's Warbler nestlings are given in Table 33.

Ten unfed nestlings at hatching weighed 1.2 g each. The average weight of 17 nestlings (some had been fed) during their first few hours of life was 1.39 ± 0.19 g (range, 1.2 g to 1.8 g). A group of 20 nestlings 24-hours-old had an average weight of 2.58 ± 0.302 g (range, 2.0 g to 3.5 g). When 48 hours old, a group of 17 nestlings had an average weight of 3.55 ± 1.08 g (range, 2.8 g to 5.0 g). When 72 hours old, a group of 11 nestlings had an average weight of 5.17 ± 0.46 g (range, 4.7 g to 6.4 g). When 96 hours old, a group of 12 nestlings had an average weight of 6.33 ± 0.89 g (range, 5.0 g to 7.6 g). When 120 hours old, a group of 10 nestlings had an average weight of 8.6 ± 1.14 g (range, 7.2 g to 10.6 g). When 144 hours old, a group of nine nestlings had an average weight of 10.24 ± 0.87 g (range, 9.3 g to 11.6 g). When 168 hours old, a group of eight nestlings had an average weight 10.96 ± 0.36 g (range, 10.2 g to 11.3 g). When 192 hours old, a group of six nestlings had an average weight of 11.63 ± 0.95 g (range, 10.0 g to 12.9 g). When 216 hours old, three nestlings had an average weight of 11.87 ± 0.76 g (range, 11.2 g to 12.7 g). Table 33 records the weights and measurements of additional birds. Most of these data were gathered in the early morning. The distribution of these weights when placed on a graph resembles the one presented by Mayfield (1960:109).

TABLE 33. Weights and Measurements[1] of Nestling Kirtland's Warblers at Different Ages.

Age (Days)	N	Weight (g)	Length (mm)				
			Wing Chord	Longest Primary	Tarsus	Exposed Culmen	Tail
Hatching Day	21	1.44 (1.2–1.9)	6.63 (6.0–7.0)	0.0	6.07 (5.0–7.0)	3.02 (3.0–4.0)	0.0
1	24	2.48 (1.8–3.5)	7.83 (7.0–9.0)	0.0	7.41 (6.0–9.0)	3.87 (3.0–5.0)	0.0
2	21	3.57 (2.2–5.0)	10.0 (9.0–12.0)	trace	9.50 (8.5–11.0)	4.12 (3.0–5.0)	0.0
3	16	5.20 (4.6–6.4)	12.75 (10.0–16.0)	3.0	10.87 (9.0–13.0)	5.03 (4.0–7.0)	0.0
4	14	6.39 (5.0–7.6)	15.89 (12.0–20.0)	4.75 (3.0–7.0)	12.75 (11.0–14.0)	5.56 (4.0–7.5)	0.0

TABLE 33. Continued

Age (Days)	N	Weight (g)	Length (mm)				
			Wing Chord	Longest Primary	Tarsus	Exposed Culmen	Tail
5	24	7.37 (7.2–10.6)	21.77 (14.0–27.0)	8.99 (6.0–15.5)	15.20 (12.0–17.0)	7.00 (4.0–7.5)	0.0
6	43	9.77 (8.3–11.6)	27.11 (19.0–32.0)	12.89 (12.0–20.0)	16.85 (15.0–18.5)	8.15 (7.0–11.0)	0.0
7	24	10.96 (10.2–11.3)	30.00 (28.0–33.0)	15.50 (13.0–20.0)	18.37 (17.0–19.0)	8.00 ( )	0.0
8	21	11.28 (10.0–11.9)	34.23 (32.1–38.0)	17.83 (14.0–21.0)	19.16 (18.0–21.0)	8.16 (8.0–9.0)	0.0
9	5	11.98 (11.2–12.7)	41.44 (38.9–45.0)	22.00 (20.0–25.0)	21.60 (20.0–21.8)	9.43 (8.1–10.0)	5.8 (2.0–9.2)
10	7	11.0 (1)	41.14 (39.0–42.0)	24.00	19.50 (1)	9.10 (1)	9.1
12	1		53.0		22.0	11.0	12.0
37	1		64.7				61.0
40	1	(male)	68.5				56.9

[1] Averages; ranges given in parentheses.

Hatching

The last egg in a clutch was normally laid later in the morning than previous eggs and it usually hatched a day later than the other eggs. Most eggs hatched during the daytime, but a few did hatch at night. In two nests all of the eggs hatched during a 10 hour period, while other nests required 25 hours for all of the eggs to hatch. I never observed a nest that required more than 25 hours for all of the eggs to hatch. The recorded data for 14 nests include the dates of hatching of the first and last eggs in the clutch (all eggs in the clutch hatched). The time periods required for all eggs to hatch were: 2 hours (3 yg), 8 hours (2 yg, 3 yg), 9 hours (4 yg, 4 yg, 4 yg), 10 hours (5 yg, 4 yg), 11 hours (5 yg, 3 yg), 22–25 hours (5yg, 5yg, 5yg, 5yg). The average period of time required was 12.6 hours.

Several extremes in the length of hatching time are recorded. In 1944 at Nest 1, the fifth egg was laid on 6 June. The exact time of laying was not known, but all previous eggs had been laid in early morning. On 19 June at 0600 hrs EST the nest still contained five eggs. At 0700 hrs EST there were three nestlings, and by 1700 hrs EST the nest contained five nestlings. The eggs had all hatched in less than 11 hours and required an incubation period of about 320 hours (13 days). In 1970 at Nest 5, there were four warbler eggs and one cowbird egg. The four warbler eggs hatched, but the cowbird egg did not. On 19 June at 0500 hrs EST there were four eggs, at 1200 hrs EST there were two nestlings, and at 1500 hrs there were four nestlings. These four eggs hatched during a 10 hour period. In 1973 at Nest 2, five eggs were laid between 31 May and 4 June and one egg disappeared on 15–16 June. On 16 June at 1600 hrs EST the eggs were measured. In the early morning of 17 June there were three nestlings and one egg. The fourth nestling was found during the early morning of 18 June.

Behavior

The behavior of Kirtland's Warbler nestlings has been extensively described by Mayfield (1960). One-hour-old nestlings, if unbrooded, struggle to support themselves, raise their heads, and open their mouths for food. They show no fear until they are six days old after which they show it regularly. From six to eight days of age the nestlings cower in the bottom of the nest if a hand reaches for them. When the nestlings reach eight and nine days of age, it is difficult to keep them in the nest. When the nestlings reach the fledgling stage, nine to ten days after hatching, their coloration is streaked light gray, dark gray and white. They somewhat resemble a closed jack pine cone even matching the color of the pine branches. A fledgling sitting motionless on a jack pine branch with its bill pointing upwards greatly resembles a jack pine cone.

Newly hatched warblers utter low, sibilant calls which are barely audible at a distance of a few meters. When the nestlings are six to ten days old, they often simultaneously utter a rapid twittering, *'tee-tee-tee-tee-tee'*. The volume of this call is loud enough to be heard by predators. After the nestlings fledge, they give rapid chipping calls, but soon crawl into hiding and chip only when hungry.

Parental Care

During the period of incubation and the first seven nights of the nestling period, the female remains on the nest throughout the night unless she is frightened. On 23 June 1938 I visited Nest 3 at 2100 hrs EST as darkness was falling. Neither parent was brooding the eight-day-old nestlings. On 21 July 1944 I spent all night in a blind one meter from a nest containing four eight- or nine-day-old nestlings and neither parent spent the night there. I am quite sure my presence did not keep the adults away. On the days when the first two eggs were laid, no female was found on a nest after the eggs were laid in the morning. On 15 visits to nests when the third egg was laid, females were found on five occasions. After the fourth egg was laid, the female was found on the nest 10 times in 16 visits. On the day the fifth egg was laid, the female was found on the nest only four times in 11 visits. During visits to nests during the incubation period, females were found on the nest 199 times (88.4%). These data agree with the previous report by Mayfield (1960) that female Kirtland's Warblers spend 80% to 88% of their time incubating eggs. It should be noted, however, that most of my visits occurred during the early morning when females probably incubated more frequently due to cooler temperatures. A detailed description of the incubation routine can be found in Mayfield (1960).

The amount of brooding decreased throughout the nestling period as the thermoregulatory ability of the nestlings improved and as their food demand increased. The numbers of times females were found brooding compared with the total number of visits to the nest for specific days were: day of hatching—26 of 29 (89.7%); day one—25 of 26 (90.2%); day two—26 of 26 (100%); day three—18 of 20 (90%); days four and five—15 of 17 (88.2%); day six—9 of 17 (52.9%); day seven—3 of 21 (14.4%); day eight—2 of 28 (7.1%); days nine and ten—1 of 60 (1.7%). The amount of time spent brooding also depended on weather conditions. If the weather was cold or rainy, the female (and occasionally the male) stopped periodically to brood, regardless of the age of the nestlings.

The female searched for food within an area 91 m to 122 m of the nest. Frequently, she left the nest when the singing male approached, indicating that his actions may have induced her to begin foraging. When she left the nest, she sometimes flew beneath the leafy branches, but more often she flew to a nearby branch and then gradually moved into the denser middle branches. The adults fed on insects such as larvae, moths, flies, small beetles, and cicadas which were brought back to the nestlings. Females have also been observed eating small red ants which invaded the nest in their absence. They even stood for some time picking these ants off the nestlings. During the second nesting period parents may bring blueberries to their nestlings and, after squeezing out the juice, offer them the pulp. During the early part of the nestling period, when the female is engaged primarily in brooding, the male provided much of the nestlings' food.

If a neighboring male warbler or other small bird such as a Chipping Sparrow, Field Sparrow, or Chickadee came close to the nest, the female dashed off the nest and chased it away (in cases where the male was absent). When a larger bird such as a Blue Jay or a mammal such as a thirteen-lined ground squirrel came within one meter of the nest, the female went into her distraction display. She flew slowly ahead just over the ground cover with fluttering wings and often with a spread or half-spread tail showing the white in the outer tail feathers.

Males continue to defend their territories during the incubation and brooding periods, but the vigor of the defense decreases. Males continue singing, but only occasionally from lofty perches. More often, they sing from inside densely grown regions of jack pines. During the period when nestlings are extremely small, the female must brood them almost continuously. At this time, the male brings the greatest amount of food to the nestlings. However, he still does not allow neighboring males to encroach upon his territory and must make some excursions around his territory even when busy with food gathering.

During incubation time, some males regularly feed their mates on the nest while others never do so. Mayfield (1960) reported great individual variability in this behavior. He recorded six males that fed their incubating mates only 24 times during 46 hrs and 14 min of observation. I have observed males carrying food to the female on the nest, but because of my proximity the males sometimes held the food in their beak for as long as 15 min before feeding the females. The male frequently circled his territorial boundaries while the female incubated. Periodically, he passed near the nest, singing as he came. As he neared the nest, the female left and began to feed accompanied by the male. The male often stopped singing entirely until the female was back on the nest. A male who is disturbed near the nest will often assume a motionless stance so as not to give away the nest location. I have seen males remain in this "frozen" position for as long as five minutes. Almost always the female was found on the nest directly below the spot where the male stood.

The male usually seemed to know when the eggs hatched, since he immediately began bringing insects much smaller than those he brought to the

TABLE 34. Age of Fledgling Kirtland's Warblers at Last Parental Feeding.

Year & Nest No.	Region & Section	Date Nestlings Fledged	No. of Nestlings	Date last seen fed by a parent & which parent	No. of Fledglings Present	Age of Fledglings in days	No. found in later years
1974-2	LMA-5	25 June	5	19 July M	3	34	1 F
1974-6	LMA-5	24 June	4	22 July M	3	38	1 M*
1974-10	LMA-5	26 June	5	22 July M	4	36	0
1974-24	LMA-5	25 June	5	22 July M	4	37	2 F
1974-32	LMA-5	21 June	3+	22 July M	1+	41	0
1975-6	LMA-5	23 June	5	22 July M	5	39	1 F
1976-7	LMA-5	19 June	5	15 July M, F	5	36	1 F
				18 July F	2	39	
1976-10	LMA-5	25 June	4	13 July M, F	3	28	0
1976-12	LMA-5	25 June	4	15 July M, F	4	30	0
1976-16	ARN-8	18 June	4	18 July** M	1		1 M
1976-20	LMA-5	4 July	5	20 July M, F	5	26	0
Mean		24 June	4.45	20 July 11 M 5 F	3.45	34.8	2 M 5 F

*this male was found during 1978 in Quebec
**this fledgling was feeding on its own, but the male was near. This same fledgling was captured the following year. All adults were color banded and all nestlings were wearing one aluminum band.

female. During this time, he brought food to the nest every few minutes. As the nestlings became older, both parents shared more equally in the feeding duties. On 26 June 1974 parents were observed feeding four seven-day-old nestlings. During a 45 min period, the male fed them twice and he also brought food three other times which he gave to the female who, in turn, gave it to the nestlings. The female fed the nestlings nine other times. Thus, each nestling was fed on an average of once every 13.1 min. In 1944 at Nest 3 parents fed four nine-day-old nestlings every 10 min for an entire afternoon while we photographed them. They collected large larvae some of which were mashed on branches before being fed to the nestlings. Before the day was over, they also fed the nestlings portions of ripe blueberries.

Van Tyne observed the rates of feeding at three nests (Mayfield 1960). At one nest each of two cowbirds was fed every 18.4 min on the day of hatching. At another nest a pair fed two three-day-old warblers every 54.8 min, while the next day they fed them every 48.6 min (observation time, 630 min and 195 min, respectively). At a third nest each of two six-day-old warblers was fed every 16.6 min (observation time, 240 min). When five nestlings were present, both parents fed them 20 times in 150 min of observation, thus, each nestling received food every 37.5 min. On the next day, when these nestlings were nine days old, both parents fed them 72 times during 250 min, thus, each nestling was fed every 17.4 min. During these six periods of observation, the male fed the nestlings 106 times and the female fed them 72 times. Fecal sacs were removed two, six, three, nine, four and eleven times during these six periods of observation. The parents devoured the fecal sacs while the nestlings were quite young, but later they dropped them on the ground or wiped them on a branch 30 m or more from the nest.

A female who renested after a successful first nest had the major responsibility at the second nest for a period of time while the male cared for the fledglings from the first nest. If the female did not renest, then both parents cared for the fledglings. Observations were made on 10 broods to determine how long the parents fed them. The male fed the brood in six families, the female fed the brood in one family, and both parents fed the fledglings in the remaining three families. In 1974 at Nest 8 the female fed the nestlings with the male on 20 June. The next morning only the male was there (observation time, 90 min). The nestlings were ready to fledge and did so during that period. Even in the single case where the female was in charge of the family, the male had shared caretaking responsibility with her until three days prior to this observation. Fledglings were fed by parents until they were 26–41 days old ($\bar{x}$ = 34.8 days) (Table 34). Several fledglings were independent by 38–40 days. Observations of 11 warbler families are summarized in Table 34. These 11 families produced 49 fledglings, all from first nestings ($\bar{x}$ = 4.45 nestlings). One month later, these 11 sets of parents were observed with at least 38 fledglings ($\bar{x}$ = 3.45 fledglings).

CHAPTER 11

NESTING SUCCESS

Mortality of Adults

During the period 1931–1978, I observed the actual death of only two adult Kirtland's Warblers, both female. On 4 July 1941 a female warbler was incubating her five eggs at both 0630 hrs and 1600 hrs EST. On 5 July at 0500 hrs EST the nest was empty and feathers were strewn around the area. A new house had been built a few hundred meters away among the small jack pines and the predator apparently was a house cat. On 13 June 1978 a female Kirtland's Warbler was observed incubating six eggs. On 16 June the eggs were cold and no female was found. A short search revealed a neat pile of feathers where a predator had devoured the bird. The nest and eggs were intact. The nest was located only 13 m from a gravel highway and again, the predator apparently was a house cat.

Two males, their mates, and families were never relocated after a forest fire in early July 1976 in the shelling zone near Kyle Lake, Crawford County. The forest fire on the Artillery Range North occurred just before the spring arrival of male Kirtland's Warblers and two of three males that had been banded the year before were found there. They moved onto the Artillery Range South. If the two Kyle Lake families succeeded in escaping the fire, they were never found again.

Nolan (1978) in studying Prairie Warblers found that if they survived their first summer and winter, they usually lived for many years. This same tendency was seen in my studies with banded adult Kirtland's Warblers and with returning warblers banded the year after they were hatched (Table 35).

Loss of Eggs and Nestlings

The reason that eggs or nestlings disappeared from a nest was usually not known. The nest rarely showed signs of violence, but was simply empty; eggshells or the remains of nestlings were not usually found. However, on two occasions nests were torn out of their location and scattered about. At one of these locations a skunk and raccoons had been observed. At the sec-

TABLE 35.   Survival of Kirtland's Warblers, 1964–1982.

Age When Banded, Sex	Years Found After Banding									Total		Estimated Age and Standard Deviation
	1	2	3	4	5	6	7	8	9	Birds	Years	
AHY, ♂ ♂	26	7	14	5	2	4	2	3	0	63	174	2.76 ± 2.06
AHY, ♀ ♀	43	6	6	3	2	1	1	0	0	62	108	1.74 ± 1.38
N, ♂ ♂	1	7	3	6	4	4	1	0	1	27	108	4.00 ± 1.90
N, ♀ ♀	7	6	4	0	1	0	2	0	0	20	50	2.50 ± 1.85
Total	77	26	27	14	9	9	6	3	1	172	440	2.56 ± 1.93

AHY = Birds of unknown age, at least one year old when banded.
N = Birds banded as nestlings.

ond location several crows had been seen. However, there is no proof that any of these animals actually destroyed the nests.

There are two documented cases of Blue Jay predation on Kirtland's Warblers. In the first, a Blue Jay was observed beating the head of an eight-day-old warbler nestling with its beak. Three nest mates of the victim had rapidly scattered into the surrounding vegetation and the parents and a pair of Chipping Sparrows were hanging in midair 30 cm above the nest location, beating their wings rapidly. The nestling which was attacked by the Blue Jay died within several minutes of the assault. The remaining three nestlings escaped harm. On 1 July 1967 at 1200 hrs EST, two nestling cowbirds were observed in Nest 1. The parents were feeding them regularly. Fifteen minutes later a Blue Jay was observed sitting on the edge of the nest eating the last cowbird nestling. The Blue Jay flew off into the forest leaving the nest empty. Since Brown-headed Cowbirds have been removed from Kirtland's Warbler nesting regions, the Blue Jay has become the warbler's worst predator, found on nearly all warbler territories. An investigation of other species of birds and mammals found on 100 different warbler territories showed the Blue Jay to be the single most prevalent species. It was found on 86 of the 100 territories studied (Table 36).

The thirteen-lined ground squirrel is probably the next most serious predator of the Kirtland's Warbler. William Freeman (personal communication) and Leighton Smith (verbal communication) both observed this mammal dragging nestlings from the nest. Although they interfered with this predation, the nests were empty on the following day. Field observations indicate that ground squirrels do not take all of the nest contents at one time. Part of a clutch or several nestlings usually disappear one day, and the remainder are taken on a future day.

Red squirrels are also suspected of preying on Kirtland's Warblers. On

10 July 1970 at Nest 18, a red squirrel was seen within 1 m of the nest. This sighting occurred at 0500 hrs EST and the nest contents were intact; at 0600 hrs EST the two nestling cowbirds had vanished. A small burrow could be seen in the bottom of the nest. On 21 June 1975 at Nest 3, four small nestlings were observed. On 23 June only one nestling remained and a pine cone had been added. The next day only the pine cone remained. This case of predation was probably also the work of a red squirrel.

One documented case of garter snake predation on Kirtland's Warblers is also recorded. On 27 June 1972 at Nest 25, a pair of Kirtland's Warblers and their five nestlings were banded. On 1 July O. S. Pettingill (personal communication) visited the region and found this pair of adult warblers in an agitated state. The nest was empty and nearby a large garter snake was found which showed several lumps in its body. Three of the banded nestlings

TABLE 36.   Number of Times Other Animals Occupied the Same Territory as 100 Pairs of Kirtland's Warblers. (100 territories
were included in this study)

Blue Jay	86	Nighthawk	5
Chipping Sparrow	49	Tree Swallow	5
Vesper Sparrow	34	Black-capped Chickadee	5
Brown Thrasher	28	American Robin	5
Brewer's Blackbird	17	Eastern Bluebird	5
Lincoln's Sparrow	17	Pine Warbler	5
Nashville Warbler	15	Woodland jumping mouse	4
Field Sparrow	15	Common Flicker	4
Thirteen-lined ground		Yellow-rumped Warbler	4
squirrel	14	Clay-colored Sparrow	3
Prairie Warbler	12	Mourning Dove	2
Snowshoe hare	11	Black-backed Three-	
Rufous-sided Towhee	10	toed Woodpecker	2
White-throated Sparrow	9	Sharp-tailed Grouse	2
Red squirrel	8	Western Palm Warbler	2
Upland Sandpiper	8	Eastern Meadowlark	2
Song Sparrow	8	Mallard	1
American Kestrel	7	Spruce Grouse	1
American Crow	7	Striped skunk	1
Cedar Waxwing	7	Raccoon	1
Sharp-shinned Hawk	6	Rose-breasted Grosbeck	1
Northern Junco	6		

Whitetail deer, porcupines, and coyotes roamed most regions continuously. Marsh Hawks and Bald Eagles flew regularly over many regions and cowbirds formerly occurred on all territories. These counts were made at the Artillery Range South, the Lovells Management Area, and Muskrat Lake.

were squeezed out of the snake and a fourth was found dead beside the nest. The fifth nestling was not located.

At several nests female Kirtland's Warblers have been observed removing small, dark red ants from the nestlings and from the edge of the nest and its vicinity. The birds ate the ants. Large red ant mounds are found in most warbler territories, but there is no proof that they cause the birds any trouble.

Tables 37 and 38 record losses of Kirtland's Warbler eggs and nestlings. During the 12 year period, 1966–1977, 282 nests were observed and 179 of these nests had nestling Kirtland's Warblers fledge from them (63.5%). A total of 1,093 warbler eggs were observed in these nests of which 787 hatched (72.0%) and 657 nestlings fledged (60.1%). Almost 40% of the warbler eggs never reached the fledged nestling stage. Eighty-five eggs failed to hatch (7.8%). The greatest losses were accounted for by the 169 eggs and 95 nestlings taken by predators (24.2%).

Table 38 shows the days when eggs or nestlings disappeared during the Kirtland's Warbler nesting cycle. Five eggs were taken and seven were deserted during laying time. The duration of the laying period is normally five days, thus 2.4 eggs were lost per day. During the 14-day incubation period, 133 eggs were lost or 9.5 eggs per day. During the nine-day nestling period, 81 nestlings were lost to predators or 9 nestlings per day. If the 9 nestlings which died of natural causes are added to this total, then 10 nestlings were lost per day. Of the 971 eggs laid during the period 1972–1977, 615 eggs are known to have produced fledged nestlings. Two hundred thirty-five of the remaining 356 eggs were lost and the date of this loss was recorded. This leaves 121 eggs (95 eggs, 26 nestlings) for which the exact date of loss is not recorded. Assuming these 121 losses would have occurred at the same rate as the recorded losses, then 6 eggs (5.11%) would have been lost during the laying period, 68 eggs (56.6%) during the incubation period, 42 eggs (34.5%) during the nestling period, and five nestlings (3.8%) would have died.

The evidence derived from the return rate of adult birds, from the known life spans of individual birds, and from the present nesting success indicates that the greatest mortality of Kirtland's Warblers occurs during the nine months when the species is outside Michigan. Sixty-three percent of the warblers that leave Michigan never return (Table 39). The tremendous loss of warblers between 1973 and 1974 (216 singing males in 1973 as compared with 167 singing males in 1974) could have been the result of a hurricane that swept through the Bahamas in October 1973.

Kirtland's Warblers undoubtedly suffer in many regions because of development causing decreased habitat. Three examples of such losses are the male that flew into a picture window in Cincinnati, the bird that flew into a lighthouse at Put-in-Bay, Ohio, and another bird that flew into a lighthouse at Mackinac City, Michigan. Very little is known about the food require-

TABLE 37. Losses of Kirtland's Warbler Eggs and Nestlings, 1966–1977.

Year	1966	1967	1968	1969	1970	1971	1972	1973	1974	1975	1976	1977	Total
Number of Nests	7	6	1	9	16	13	32	34	63	37	33	31	282
Number Successful	1	2	0	3	7	6	22	23	47	26	23	19	179
Number of KW Eggs Observed	4	13	4	24	48	29	135	150	258	162	134	132	1,093
KWs Hatched	2	5	0	6	27	16	106	115	200	119	104	87	787
KWs Fledged	2	5	0	6	17	12	87	92	181	102	89	64	657
Total Eggs Lost	2	8	4	18	21	13	29	35	58	43	30	45	306
Total Nestlings Lost	0	0	0	0	10	4	19	23	19	17	15	23	130
Eggs Possibly Hatched					(6	3	3	4	2				18E)
Eggs Failed to Hatch	1	1	0	1	8	1	12	9	16	14	10	12	85E
KW Eggs & Yg. Apparently Taken by cowbird	1E			2E	6E	4E			1Y				13E 1Y
Deserted Eggs		3		4	3		7	3	6				26E
Predator Removed (1) Eggs		4	4	5	4	5	10	22	34	29	20	32	169E
(2) Nestlings						4	14	18	17	16	9	17	95Y
Eggs or Young Disappeared					1Y			1E			1Y	2Y	1E 4Y
Unknown				6E	9Y	3E	2	4Y	2E	1		1E	12E 16Y
Nestlings Died								1	1	1	5	4	14Y

TABLE 38. Day of Loss of Kirtland's Warbler Eggs and Nestlings, 1972–1977.

Year	Laying									Incubation Period (Eggs)													Nesting Period						Total
	1	2	3	4	5	6	7	8	9	10	11	12	13	14	15	16	17	18	19	20	21	22	23	24	25	26	27	28	
1972								5				5											3		5	1	5		10 eggs 14 yg.
1973		2									5	4	4			4		4	3	2	1	5				5	5		26 eggs 18 yg.
1974		2		4D									4			5	5	10		3				3				1	26 eggs 4D 7 yg.
1975									5		9	5				4		4	5	3	4				5			4	28 eggs 16 yg.
1976	1		3D							4			5				5	2		1			6	1	1	(5)			17 eggs 3D 9 yg. 5 died
1977											4			5		9	8		5		5			(2)	2 (2)			10	31 eggs 17 yg. 4 died
Total	1	4	3	4				5	5	4	18	14	13	5		18	18	20	13	9	10	5	9	4 (2)	13 (2)	6 (5)	10	15	145 eggs 9 died 81 young

D = deserted
( ) = young died
Table includes only actual known losses.

TABLE 39. Annual Survival of Kirtland's Warbler.

	First Nesting				Second Nesting						
Year	No. of Pairs	No. of Eggs Laid x̄ = 4.78	No. of Nestlings Fledged	No. of Young One Month after Fledging	No. of Pairs	No. of Eggs Laid x̄ = 4.00	No. of Nestlings Fledged	No. of Young One Month after Fledging	Total Fall Count if No More Lost	Returns the Next Spring	Lost During Nine Months
1972	200	956	605	471	100	400	253	197	1,068	432	636
1973	216	1,032	654	508	108	432	273	213	1,153	334	819
1974	167	798	505	393	83.5	334	211	164	891	358	533
1975	179	856	542	421	89.5	358	227	176	955	400	555
1976	200	956	605	471	100	400	253	197	1,068	436	632
1977	218	1,042	660	513	109	436	276	215	1,164	392	772
Total	1,180	5,640	3,571	2,777	590	2,360	1,493	1,162	6,299	2,352	3,947

ments of this bird, especially during the migration and on the wintering grounds. In Michigan the food supply appears to be adequate. However, as more and more people in Michigan build their second homes near warbler habitat and bring their pets with them, a definite impact will be felt on the warbler population. The future of this species is by no means secure.

Nesting Success

Although it is impossible to find all nests of any species, the outcome of those nests that are found probably reflects the percentage of success of all nests. Of 67 Kirtland's Warbler nests found when the female was building or laying eggs, the eggs hatched in 41 nests (61.2%) and the nestlings fledged from 32 nests (47.8%). Two hundred ninety warbler eggs were observed in these 67 nests of which 164 hatched (56.6%) and 125 nestlings fledged (43.1%). Thirty-six nests were found between the second day of incubation (known) and the first day of hatching. Twenty-five of these nests had eggs hatch (69.4%) and young fledged from 20 nests (55.6%). One hundred fifty-eight warbler eggs were observed in these 36 nests of which 99 hatched (62.7%) and 80 nestlings fledged (50.6%). One hundred five nests were found containing nestlings. Ninety of these nests had nestlings fledge (85.7%). Four hundred thirty-one nestlings and eggs were observed in these 105 nests of which 391 hatched (90.7%) and 340 nestlings fledged (78.9%).

A combination of these three groups yields a total of 208 nests. Eggs hatched in 171 nests (82.2%) and nestlings fledged from 142 nests (68.3%). Eight hundred seventy-nine eggs or nestlings were observed in these 208 nests of which 545 nestlings fledged (62.0%). These data show that the period when a nest was found affects the statistical determination of nesting success.

Animals in the Nesting Habitat

The following animals have been found in Kirtland's Warbler nesting regions:

> Raccoon (*Procyon lotor*)
> Striped skunk (*Mephitis mephitis*)
> Badger (*Taxidea taxus*)
> Red fox (*Vulpes fulva*)
> Coyote (*Canis latrans*)
> Woodchuck (*Marmota monax*)
> Thirteen-lined ground squirrel (*Citellus tridecemlineatus*)
> Red squirrel (*Tamiasciurus hudsonicus*)

Meadow jumping mouse (*Zapus hudsonius*)
Porcupine (*Erethizon dorsatum*)
Snowshoe hare (*Lepus americanus*)
Whitetail deer (*Odocoileus virginianus*)
Garter snake (*Thamnophis sirtalis*)
Smooth green snake (*Opheodrys vernalis*)
Hognosed snake (*Heterodon platyrhinos*)

CHAPTER 12

INDIVIDUAL HISTORIES

Individual Histories of Banded Nestlings

These histories deal with banded nestlings found during the years 1968–1981 (Table 13 and 14):

Male 1 (75-36698). This male was one of four nestlings banded on 1 July 1969 on the Artillery Range South. In July 1971 he was captured by Bruce Radabaugh at Mack Lake, Oscoda County, 43 km from the Artillery Range South. He returned to Mack Lake in 1972 and 1973.

Male 2 (116-24662). This bird was banded by Bruce Radabaugh in early July 1971 at Mack Lake, Oscoda County. He was captured at Lovells Management Area on 28 May 1973 and color banded. He and his mate (820-89201) fledged four nestlings from five eggs on 27–28 June 1973. In 1974 he mated with Female 81-58978 and five nestlings fledged on 24 June. A cowbird laid an egg in their second nest. When I found this nest it contained only two eggs, the cowbird egg and one warbler egg. Although the warbler egg hatched, something dragged the newly hatched nestling out of the nest and removed its legs. The cowbird nestling remained untouched. On 23 June 1975 this male and his unbanded mate produced five fledged nestlings. This male was killed at Cincinnati, Ohio, on 27 September 1975. The specimen was saved and is in the collection of the U.S. National Museum in Washington, D.C.

Male 5 (81-58909). This male was among the five nestlings that hatched on 11–12 June 1972. All five nestlings fledged between 0830 hrs and 1000 hrs on 21 June. Male 5 settled 1.6 km north of his natal nest in 1973 (Artillery Range North). His mate was Female 820-89263 and they produced four fledged nestlings on 1 July. Male 5 was still found on an adjacent territory in June 1977.

Male 6 (81-58913). This bird fledged with four nest mates from Nest 19 on the Lovells Management Area on 23 June 1972. During 1973 he mated with a one-year-old female (Female 8/81-58978) and they nested 460 m north of his birthplace and 183 m from her birthplace. She laid four eggs on 17–20 June of which two hatched on 3 July and fledged on 13 July. The next year Male 6 did not return, but Female 8 mated with Male 2 on the same territory. On 25 June 1981 Matt Anderson found Male 6 on the Artillery Range North mated with an unbanded female. Five nestlings fledged. This male was nine years old and the two areas where he nested are 14.5 km apart.

Male 7 (81-58930). One of five nestlings, this bird fledged on 25 June 1972 at Lovells Management Area. He was color banded on this territory in 1973, but no nest was found. In 1974 and 1975 his mate was Female 6 (81-58914), a returning female. They lost their first nest each year and renested in late June. They produced two fledged nestlings from five eggs on 1 August 1974 and four nestlings from five eggs on 29 July 1975. The territory occupied by Male 7 in 1974 and 1975 was very large and was located 1.2 km from his birthplace. While mist-netting birds 1.6 km south of this territory on 22 July 1974, I captured this male even though his mate was incubating eggs. In both 1976 and 1977 he nested in this same region, but never returned to his old territory.

In 1976 Male 7 mated with Female 17 (830-20555), one of his brother's offsprings. Five nestlings fledged on 25 June. This was the second time in five nestings that all his eggs had hatched and fledged. Four eggs in their second nest hatched, but the nestlings were taken by a predator on 25 July. During 1977 Male 7 was mated with Female 880-52640. Four of her five eggs hatched, but only two fledged on 23 June. I found no sign of a second nest. During 1978 Male 7 mated with Female 860-40320 and five young fledged on 28 June. Much of the time Male 7 nested at Lovells his mother, a brother, and three sisters also nested there. Male 7 was the father of 18 nestlings that fledged successfully.

Males 9 and 10 (81-58944 and 81-58947, brothers). These birds fledged on 25 June 1972 on the Artillery Range South. Female 81-58948 also fledged from the same nest. Male 9 was found at Muskrat Lake, Oscoda County, 21 km from his birthplace in June 1973 by Warren Faust. In 1975 he produced five fledged nestlings (Craig Orr, verbal communication), but was not found subsequently. Male 10 was found on the Artillery Range North, 1.6 km from his birthplace. Although I never searched for his nest, he was on the Artillery Range North from 1973 through 1976.

Male 12 (81-58962). This bird's father (61-24195) and mother (81-58943) nested on the Artillery Range South. Five young fledged on 28 June 1972 during the third summer I had observed Male 61-24195. Male 12 was found in 1973 on the Artillery Range North, 1.38 km north of his birthplace, but his nest was not located. On this same territory he and his left-banded mate produced four fledged nestlings on 26 June 1974 at 1600 hrs. A cowbird egg laid in their nest proved to be infertile. During 1975 Male 12 mated with an unbanded female and several young fledged in late June. In 1976 Male 12 and an unbanded female produced four fledged nestlings from five eggs on 18 June. During 1977 he mated with Female 880-52613 and five nestlings fledged on 21 June. In 1978 Male 12 was located at the extreme northern edge of the Artillery Range North. He was seen with an unbanded mate on 17 June who was building a nest. This nest was later found deserted. *Males 13 and 14 (81-58977 and 81-58979, brothers)*. These males fledged on 26 June 1972 at Lovells Management Area along with Female 81-58978. Male 13 nested 395 m from his birthplace in 1973. This nest had two eggs on 3 July which were taken by a predator. In 1974 Male 13 returned to the same territory but no nest was found. In 1976 Warren Faust and I located Male 13 on 22 June at Kyle Lake; he and his mate produced two fledged nestlings on 27 June. A cowbird egg in the same nest failed to hatch. A fire raged through this region in July 1976 and the family was never located again.

Male 14 was found by Warren Faust in 1973 at Muskrat Lake, Oscoda County. In 1974 Craig Orr found his nest at Muskrat Lake from which four nestlings fledged on 25 June. In 1975 Male 14 and his unbanded mate produced five fledged nestlings on 22 June. In 1976 he and an unbanded mate produced five fledged nestlings on 23 June. In 1977 Male 14 and Female 880-52641 produced four fledged nestlings from five eggs on 25 June. All of these nests were located on the same territory. Male 14 was the father of 17 known fledged nestlings.

Male 15 (820-89206). Male 15 fledged at Lovells Management Area on 28 June 1973. Male 2 and Female 820-89201 were his parents. Warren Faust found him at Muskrat Lake, Oscoda County, in June 1974 mated to an eight-year-old female (110-09018), originally banded by Bruce Radabaugh at Mack Lake. Their five eggs were taken by a predator between 5 and 11 July. In 1975 Male 15 was found on the same territory but his nest was not located. In 1976 he moved to Lovells Management Area, Crawford County, and established a territory .8 km from his birthplace. Male 15 and Female 860-40308 produced three fledged nestlings from four eggs on 25 June. A second nest located 89 m from the first nest produced four nestlings on 25 July. In 1977 Male 15 and Female 860-40328 lost five nestlings to a predator on 29 June. They built a second nest 146 m north of the first nest. This second nest produced two fledged nestlings from three eggs on 29 July. Male 15 returned to Lovells Management Area in 1978, but his nest was not found. *Male 16 (820-89211)*. This bird was a brother of Male 7. His father was 81-58936 and his mother was 61-24179. Male 16 fledged on 28 June 1973 with four nest mates at Lovells Management Area, section 5. He established a territory 1183 m north of his birthplace on Lovells Management Area, section 6. Male 16 and his mate produced five fledged nestlings from six eggs on 26 June 1974 and four nestlings from five eggs from their second nest on 29–30 July 1974. In 1975 Male 16 had two mates. He and Female 11 (820-89252) produced three young from five eggs at a nest site .8 km from her birthplace. These young were lost to a predator before 15 June. However, Male 16 and Female 11 produced four fledged nestlings from five eggs on 23 July 1975. On the same day I found Male 16 feeding four nestlings in a nest belonging to Female 830-20532, his half-sister. These nestlings fledged the same day. Neither adult has been found in subsequent years, but Male 16's daughter (830-20555) mated with his brother in 1976.

Male 18 (820-89230). This bird was one of five nestlings fledged on 1 July 1973 at Lovells Management Area. In 1974 he mated with a one-year-old female (820-89288). They nested 229 m from her natal nest and 395 m from his natal nest. They produced four fledged nestlings from four eggs on 5 July. In 1975 the same pair produced four fledged nestlings from four eggs on 25 June. Female 820-89288 did not return in subsequent years. In 1976 Male 18 mated with Female 860-40328 and they produced four fledged nestlings from five eggs on 25 June. In 1977 Male 18 mated with an unbanded female and they lost four nestlings to a predator on 24 June. In 1978 he again mated with an unbanded female and produced six eggs. Only two eggs hatched and a predator had emptied the nest by 21 June. Male 18 returned to the same territory in 1979, but his nest was not located.

Male 21 (830-20589). This male fledged on 5 July 1974 on the Artillery Range South. His father was 820-89202 and his mother was 81-58974. Male 21 was not found in 1975. On 24 June 1976 he and an unbanded mate produced five fledged nestlings (one was Male 25). In 1977 Male 21 was mated with an unbanded female and they lost five eggs to a predator just prior to 21 June. Male 21 was not found again.

Male 25 (860-40316). This bird was the offspring of Male 21. He occupied the same territory from 1977 through 1981. During 1977 he mated with Female 5 (81-58948). He was one year old and she was five years old. They produced two fledged nestlings from five eggs on 24 June. Male 25 returned in 1978, but his nest was not located. In 1979 he mated with an unbanded female and their five eggs were taken by a predator. He returned to the same territory in both 1980 and 1981.

Male 26 (81-58970). This bird hatched on either 19 or 20 June 1972 on the Artillery Range South. Five nestlings fledged from this nest on 29 June, but none was seen again until Nancy Tilghman found two male Kirtland's Warblers at Black River Falls, Jackson County, Wisconsin. She, John Byelich, and I captured Male 26 there on 21 June 1978. We spent much of the day watching this male. We found no evidence that he was mated. A second unbanded male occupied an adjoining territory. One of these birds returned to this territory in 1979 (Nancy Tilghman, personal communication). We took several photographs of Male 26 when he was captured.

Male 27 (830-20521). Male 27 fledged on 24 June 1974 along with four other nestlings at the Lovells Management Area, Crawford County. None of these nestlings was seen again until 27 May 1978 when Male 27 was found in Quebec, 101 km east of Pembroke, Ontario, and 72 km north of Ottawa. He was found in an area where the jack pines were about 18 m tall. He was captured in a mist-net, his band number verified, and he was released (Dr. Paul Aird in a news release by G. Finney, 13 June 1978; Chamberlain and McKeating 1978). This region is 676 km east of his birthplace.

Female 1 (110-09079). This bird was banded by Bruce Radabaugh on 22 July 1967 at Mack Lake, Oscoda County. In 1972 she mated with Male 61-24176 and they nested on section 16, Artillery Range South, Crawford County. Five eggs hatched but a predator took the nestlings on 22 June. In 1974 Female 1 nested on the same territory (her probable mate was male 830-20510) and lost five eggs to a predator in June. Her 1974 nest was 142 m from her 1972 nest. Both of these nests were 43 km from her birthplace.

Female 2 (116-24628). Bruce Radabaugh banded this female at Mack Lake, Oscoda County, on 30 June 1968, just after she fledged. This female and Female 1 were undoubtedly from second nestings. On 31 May 1970 she built a nest on section 17 of the Artillery Range South, 43 km from her birthplace. Her nest eventually contained three warbler eggs and one cowbird egg. The cowbird egg was removed and three nestling warblers fledged. Her mate in 1970 was Male 61-24180.

Female 3 (116-24635). This female was banded by Bruce Radabaugh at Mack Lake, Oscoda County, on 25 June 1970. In 1972 she was found nesting at Mack Lake where she produced five fledged nestlings. In 1977 Female 3 was found at Muskrat Lake mated to Male 850-72503 (this male was banded as a nestling 97 km from Muskrat Lake by Craig Orr on 20 June 1974). Three nestlings fledged from this nest on 21 June 1977.

Female 4 (850-72516). Craig Orr banded this female on 23 June 1974 at the Pere Cheney area, Crawford County. She was found nesting on the Artillery Range North by Warren Faust and with her mate produced five fledged nestlings on 29 June 1975. Her mate was right banded but was not captured.

Female 5 (81-58948). This female along with four nest mates fledged on 25 June 1972 on the Artillery Range South. Two of her brothers (Males 9 and 10) also returned. In 1973 Female 5 was found 1.6 km east of her birthplace mated with Male 56-57414, who was at least eight years old. Five nestlings fledged on 1 July 1973. Female 5 was not found again until 1 June 1977 when she was located 1.6 km northwest of her 1973 nest site. Her mate was Male 860-40316, a one-year-old. Two nestlings fledged from five eggs (four eggs hatched) on 24 June 1977.

Female 8 (81-58978). This bird was fledged on 26 June 1972 at Lovells Management Area with two nest mates (Males 13 and 14). All three birds returned. During 1973 and 1974 Female 8 occupied the territory adjacent to her natal territory. Her father occupied her natal territory from 1972 through 1974 and her brother occupied a territory just to the south. In 1973 Female 8 mated with a one-year-old male (81-58913) and they fledged two young

from four eggs on 13 July. This nest was located only 183 m from her birthplace. In 1974 Female 8 mated with Male 2 (116-24662) when her 1973 mate did not return. Five nestlings fledged from their first 1974 nest on 25 June, but their second nest met with failure due to cowbird interference.
Females 9 and 10 (820-89228 and 820-89229). Both birds fledged on 28 June 1973 at the Lovells Management Area. Their father was 820-89214 and their mother was 81-58935. Female 9 mated with Male 81-59000 and five nestlings fledged at the Lovells Management Area on 28 June 1974. Male 81-59000 had a second mate on a second territory. In 1974 Female 9 nested 968 m from her birthplace. Female 10 was not found during 1974 or 1975. In 1976 she was found 85 m from her birthplace and with her mate, Male 860-40329, produced four fledged nestlings from four eggs on 25 June. Both parents were observed feeding these young on 13 July 1976. Male 18 (nest mate of Females 9 and 10) was found at Lovells Management Area from 1974 through 1979.
Female 11 (820-89252). This bird was the daughter of two unbanded birds and she fledged on 1 July 1973 with four nest mates. In 1975 Female 11 was found mated with Male 16 (820-89211). They lost their first nest to predators, but four nestlings fledged from their second nest on 23 July 1975.
Female 13 (820-89288). This bird was fledged on 27 July 1973 at Lovells Management Area. Her mother was 61-24179 and her father was 81-58936. Female 13 returned and nested 229 m from her birthplace. Her mate in 1974 and 1975 was Male 18 (820-89230) and the pair occupied the same territory during both summers. Female 13 and Male 18 produced four fledged nestlings on 5 July 1974 and four more on 25 June 1975. This pair did not nest for a second time either year. Their son, Male 20 (830-20584), who fledged from the 1974 nest established a territory during June 1976 near Kyle Lake (section 19, T27N, R2W), 19.3 km south of his birthplace. Before his 1976 nest was located, the region burned, apparently as a result of artillery fire. Male 20 was never found again.
Female 14 (830-20517). This bird hatched on 14 June 1974 and fledged on 24 June 1974 at Lovells Management Area, Crawford County. In 1975 she nested 743 m from her birthplace. Female 14 and her unidentified right-banded mate produced four fledged nestlings from five eggs about 30 June. During 1976 and 1977 Female 14 mated with Male 860-40390 on a territory directly adjacent to her birthplace. They lost five eggs to a predator in June 1976, but two nestlings fledged from their second nest on 9 July 1976. Five eggs were laid in their single 1977 nest from which four nestlings fledged on 27 June.
Female 15 (830-20530). This female was the daughter of Female 19 (61-24179) and Male 830-20585. She was one of five nestlings fledged on 22 June 1974 at Lovells Management Area. She returned to Lovells Management Area with the same mate in 1976 and 1977 and was probably also

there in 1975 when I was not allowed to capture Kirtland's Warblers. A right-banded female nested twice on this same territory in 1975. A predator took the five eggs from the first 1975 nest between 6 and 15 June. The second nest produced four nestlings that fledged on 11 July. Female 15 and Male 860-40301 produced five fledged nestlings on 19 June 1976 on this same territory. Both adults were observed feeding all five fledglings (in one group) 189 m from the nest site on 15 July 1976 when the young were 36 days old. On three separate days Female 15 was found feeding two fledglings 20 m farther from the nest site. One of these offsprings, Female 19 (860-40326), nested twice in 1977, 917 m from her birthplace. During 1977 Female 15 again mated with Male 860-40301 and produced four eggs of which two hatched. These nestlings fledged on 24 June. Female 15 and her mate did not attempt a second nesting in either 1976 or 1977.

Female 17 (830-20555). This bird fledged from a nest at Lovells Management Area, section 6, on 27 June 1974. Her father was Male 16 (820-89211) and her mother was 830-20518. Her paternal grandfather was 81-58936 and her paternal grandmother was 61-24179. Female 17 was not found during 1975, but in 1976 she mated with her father's brother, Male 7 (81-58930). They produced five fledged nestlings from five eggs on 25 June and then lost four nestlings from their second nest to a predator on 25 July 1975.

Female 19 (860-40326). This female was the daughter of Male 860-40301 and Female 15 (830-30530). In 1977 Female 19 mated with Male 860-40393 and nested 917 m from her birthplace at Lovells Management Area, Crawford County. She lost two clutches of eggs (five and four eggs, respectively) to predators on 12 June 1977 and on 6 July 1977. In 1978 Female 19 was found mated with an unbanded male on the Artillery Range North, section 9. Five nestlings fledged from this nest on 23 June.

Returns of Males Banded as Adults

The nesting history and location of territory for selected males banded as adults provide valuable data.

Male 38 (81-59000). All territories occupied by this male were in the northern part of section 5, Lovells Management Area, Crawford County (Figure 35). In 1972 Male 38 mated with Female 81-58999. Three nestlings fledged from their first nest on 25 June. Their second nest produced four fledged nestlings from four eggs on 27 July. In 1973 Male 38 mated with Female 820-89272. Five eggs were laid in their nest between 24 and 28 June. One egg hatched, but the nestling was taken by a predator on 13 July. In 1974 Male 38 occupied the same territory he inhabited in 1972 and 1973. His mate in 1974 was Female 830-20586. She laid four eggs between 12 and 15 June from which three nestlings fledged on 11 July. Male 38 had a second territory and a second mate in 1974. His second territory was .8 km west of his regular territory and his second mate was Female 820-89228. She laid five eggs from which five nestlings fledged on 28 June. To reach this second territory the male would fly several hundred feet up in the air and then head directly to the second territory. As it happened, nestlings were not present in both nests at the same time, but there were fledged nestlings on the second territory when there were nestlings on the first.

In 1975 Male 38 mated with an unbanded female. Four eggs were produced, but they were taken by a predator on 24 June. In 1976 Male 38 again

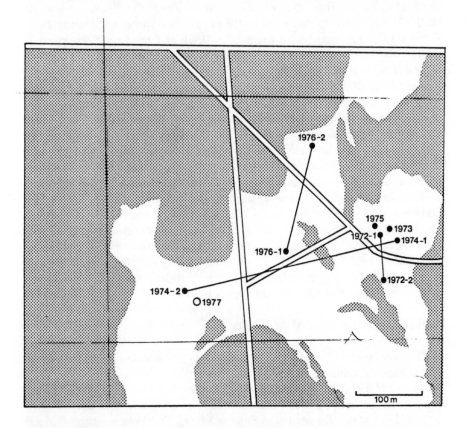

FIGURE 35.   Nests of Male 38 and His Mates During the 1972–1977 Breeding Seasons on the Lovells Management Area (Section 5, T28N, R1W). M 38 had two mates in both 1974 and 1976. He had two separate territories in 1974 (Territories 10 and 12 in Figure 25).
Stippling indicates areas of taller jack pines while clear space indicates areas of shorter jack pines suitable for nesting warblers.
Black circles = nest sites
Open circle = territory of M 38 in 1977—nest site was not found.

had two mates. Both territories were slightly north and west of his previous main territory. The first nest found was the result of a mating between Male 38 and an unbanded female. Five eggs were laid, four eggs hatched, but all the nestlings were lost to a predator. Male 38 also mated with Female 860-40369 during 1976. Their nest contained two warbler eggs and one cowbird egg, but all three were taken by a predator on 21 June. In both 1974 and 1976 I captured the male at each nest to verify these double territories. In 1977 Male 38 returned to his second 1974 territory, but he was not located after early June. During five summers he and his mates produced 15 fledged nestlings from 32 eggs (46.9%). A comparison of the nesting success of Male 38 with the nesting success of the three adult birds banded in 1966 demonstrates the efficacy of cowbird removal from the warbler habitat (Table 40).

Male 4 (112-09428). This male was banded on 30 May 1966 on the Artillery Range North by E. J. Slomkowski (personal communication). In 1970 he was located 91 m south of the area where he was banded. Four of his nests were located which contained a total of 15 warbler eggs and one cowbird egg. The cowbird egg failed to hatch, but 13 of the warbler eggs hatched and eight nestlings fledged (53.3%).

Male 6 (56-57412). This bird was banded on 4 July 1966 on the Artillery Range South. He was seven years old when last seen. Six of his nests were located containing a total of 17 eggs. Four of the six nests were parasitized by a total of eight cowbird eggs. Only 2 of the 17 warbler eggs hatched and none fledged. If they had not been removed, a total of six cowbirds would have fledged from these nests.

Male 7 (56-57414). This male was banded on 5 July 1966 on the Artillery Range North. He lost his territory in early May 1967 to fire and was not located again until 1972. During three of his eight summers four of his nests were observed. Three of these were parasitized. In these four nests only six warbler eggs were laid of which five hatched and fledged. Six cowbird eggs were observed and four of these would have fledged except for our interference (Figure 8).

Male 47 (830-20504). This male was banded on 21 June 1974 on the Artillery Range South, section 16. At this time, his mate was Female 75-36690. The female had cared for the eggs and nestlings prior to that day, but on 21 June the nest was watched for one and one-half hours and only the male was observed feeding the nestlings. These five nestlings fledged on 21 June and were still fed only by the male. Male 47 was not found in 1975, but on 24 June 1976 he was located with his unbanded mate on the same territory he had occupied in 1974. His mate laid four eggs between 27 and 30 June, but all were taken by a predator prior to 14 July. In 1981 Male 47 was found on the Artillery Range North, 1.24 km north of his 1976 territory. Richard Winters located his nest containing three eggs on 4 June. A total

TABLE 40. Kirtland's Warbler Nesting Success Before and After Removal of Adult Brown-headed Cowbirds.

Male	Age When Last Seen	No. of Nests Observed	Nest Success			Cowbird Success			
			Eggs Laid	Eggs Hatched	Young Fledged	Nests Para-sitized	Eggs Laid	Eggs Hatched	Young Fledged
112-09428	8 (1966)	4	15	13	8	1	1	0	0
56-57412	7 (1966)	6	18	2	0	4	8	6	1(6)
56-57414	8 (1966)	4	6	5	5	3	6	4	2(4)
Total	23	14	39	20	13	8	15	10	3(10)
81-58854	4 (1972)	5	19	19	13	1	1	1	1
820-89202	3 (1973)	5	24	17	14	0	0	0	0
820-89203	6 (1973)	6	28	17	12	0	0	0	0
830-20519	3 (1974)	4	19	18	13	0	0	0	0
Total	16	20	90	71	52	1	1	1	1

All seven males included in this Table were banded as adults and returned for several years. The year when each was banded is given in parentheses.

of five eggs was laid by his unbanded mate, but they were taken by a predator a few days later.

Returns of Females Banded as Adults

Female 19 (61-24179). This female is the most prolific Kirtland's Warbler I have studied (Table 41). Her nest locations are illustrated in Figures 36–41. She was first found in 1970 building a nest on the Artillery Range South, section 16 (Figure 36). She was banded on 22 June 1970. At this time, Female 19 was mated with Male 70-94978 (banded by Dr. Frank Novy on 22 June 1965 on the Artillery Range South). Their nest contained three warbler eggs and one cowbird egg. Two warbler eggs hatched after the cowbird egg was removed. These two nestlings may have fledged. Female 19 was not found in 1971, but in 1972 and in subsequent years she was found on

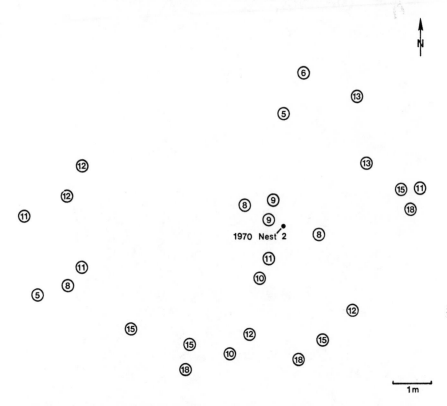

FIGURE 36.   Nest Location of Female 19 (61-24179) in 1970 (Nest 2) on the Artillery Range South (Section 16, T27N, R2W). The number inside each circle indicates the height, in feet, of the jack pine represented.

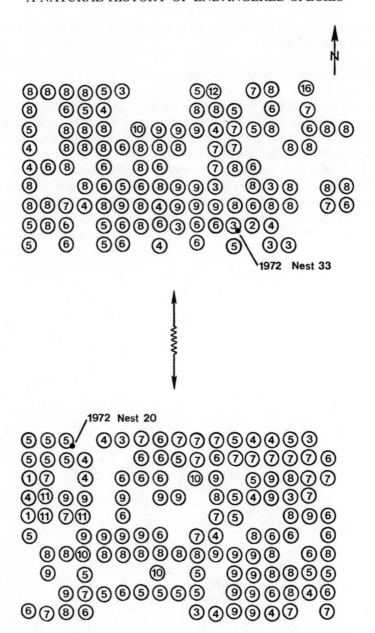

FIGURE 37.   Nest Locations of Female 19 in 1972 (Nests 20 and 33) on the Lovells Management Area (Section 5, T28N, R1W).
The number inside each circle indicates the height, in feet, of the jack pine represented.

Lovells Management Area, section 5, 15.3 km from her nesting territory on the Artillery Range South. In 1972 Female 19 was mated with Male 81-58936 and they produced five young on 25 June. This pair nested for a second time at a site 54 m northwest of their first 1972 nest (Figure 37). The four nestlings produced by this second nesting were banded and fledged on 28 July (1972 was the first year that cowbirds were trapped and removed from warbler habitat).

In 1973 Female 19 again mated with Male 81-58936 on the same territory. Their first nest contained four eggs which were laid between 2 and 5 June and which hatched on 18 June. Four nestlings fledged on 28 June. The second nesting of this pair produced three fledged nestlings on 27 July (Figure 38). Male 81-58936 did not return in 1974 and Female 19 mated with Male 830-20585 during this summer. Five nestlings fledged from their first nest on 25 June and four nestlings fledged from their second nest on 30 July (Figure 39). Neither Male 81-58936 nor Male 830-20585 returned to this territory in 1975.

Female 19 returned in 1975 to the territory she had occupied in 1972 and 1973. She mated with Male 49 (830-20519) and five nestlings fledged on 23 June. This pair apparently did not renest. In 1976 Female 19 again mated with Male 49. She laid five eggs which hatched on 16–17 June. These nestlings were found dead and partially devoured by ants on 22 June. It appeared that the female had been flushed from the nest at some time during the night since the nestlings had died of exposure. Female 19 was observed in the next row of trees south of this nest site in July, but was never seen again (Figure 40).

During the seven summers for which there are data (1971 undocumented), Female 19 laid 38 eggs of which 37 hatched and 32 nestlings fledged. Six of her offspring returned to nest on the Lovells Management Area as did two of her grandchildren. Female 19 had at least four different mates, one on the Artillery Range South (1970) and three on the Lovells Management Area (1972–1976) (Table 41, Figure 41).

The fact that Female 19 laid her eggs quite late (5–8 June) in 1970 indicates that she was probably one year old at that time. The mean laying period for first clutches of Female 19 was 30 May to 3 June and the mean date for the fledging of these nestlings was 26 June (range, 23 June to 1 July). The mean laying period for second clutches was 2 to 6 July and the mean date for the fledging of these nestlings was 28 July (range, 27 to 30 July).

In 1972 Female 19 nested on Lovells Management Area at a site 15.3 km from her 1970 nest site on the Artillery Range South. The distance between her first and second 1972 nests was 54 m; between the second 1972 nest and the first 1973 nest, 143.8 m; between the first and second 1973 nests, 32.9 m; between the second 1973 nest and the first 1974 nest, 360 m; be-

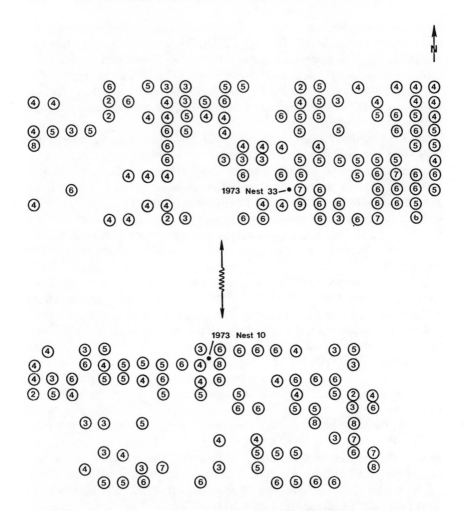

FIGURE 38.   Nest Locations of Female 19 and Male 33 in 1973 (Nests 10 and 33) on the Lovells Management Area (Section 5, T28N, R1W). The ground cover was composed of grass (*Andropogon scoparius* and *A. gerardii*) with patches of blueberries.

tween the first and second 1974 nests, 131 m; between the 1975 nest and the 1976 nest, 56.4 m. Female 19 placed her nests 3–65 cm from the base of a jack pine tree (average distance, 37.8 cm). The height of the jack pine closest to her nest varied between 1.52 m and 2.74 m (average height, 2.3 m). Female 19 often located her nest near the edge of a jack pine planting or near an opening within the planting. This pattern of nest location was commonly observed for other Kirtland's Warblers.

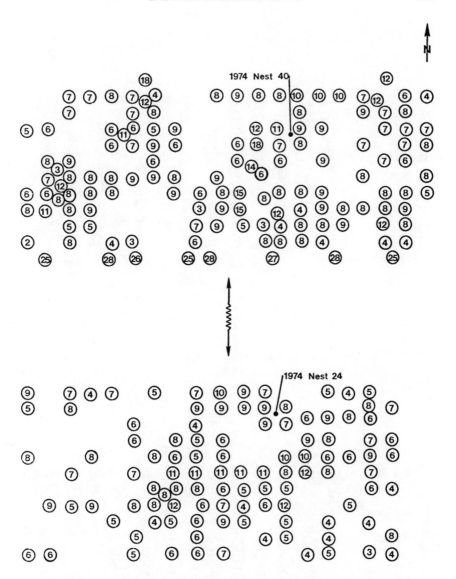

FIGURE 39. Nest Locations of Female 19 and Male 51 in 1974 (Nests 24 and 40) on the Lovells Management Area (Section 5, T28N, R1W).

Returns of Banded Nestlings

Of the 57 banded fledged nestlings from the 1977 breeding season, none has been found since, probably due to the limited time I have spent in the

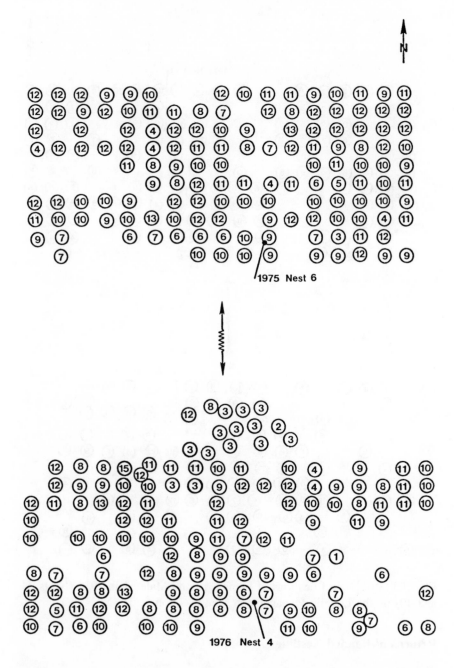

FIGURE 40.   Nest Locations of Female 19 and Male 49 in 1975 and 1976 on the Lovells Management Area (Section 5, T28N, R1W).

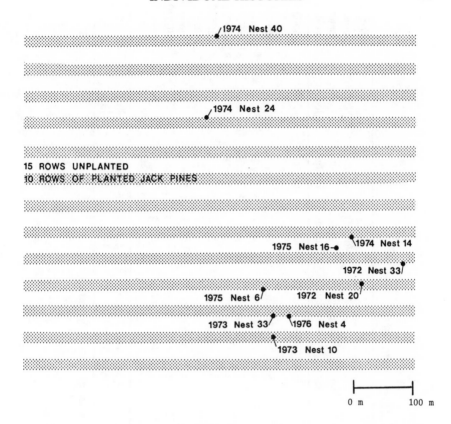

FIGURE 41. Nest Locations of Female 19 and Her Mates on the Lovells Management Area (Section 5, T28N, R1W). Nest 14 (1974) and Nest 16 (1975) belong to her daughter (820-89288). Each bar represents 10 rows of jack pines planted 1.2 m apart with 1.8 m between rows. Each 10 rows are separated by an unplanted area 15 rows (27.5 m) wide.

field since 1977. Of the 446 fledged nestlings banded prior to the 1978 season, 40 returned during later years (9.0%). These included 24 males and 16 females (Table 13 and 14). Assuming that half of the banded nestlings were male, the rate of return for male warblers banded as nestlings was 10.8% (24/223). If the 57 birds banded in 1977 are omitted, the rate of return for males was 12.3% (24/194.5). These figures for males are probably more accurate than the corresponding figures for the return of females banded as nestlings, 7.2% (including 1977) or 8.23% (excluding 1977), since females are more difficult to locate. The return rates could be higher since some birds remain undetected and at least four males, banded as nestlings on their right legs only, were never captured. The degree of site tenacity

TABLE 41. Nesting History of Female 19 (61-24179), 1970–1976.

Year	Her Mate	Region and First or Second Nest		Date Eggs were Laid	No. of Eggs	Date Eggs Hatched	No. of Eggs Hatching	Date Young Fledged	No. of Young Fledging	Nestling Returns Later Years
1970	70-94978	ARS	First	5–8 June	3 –1C	21–22 June K	2	1 July ?	2 ?*	none
1971	?	?								
1972	81-58936	LMA	First	29 May–2 June	5	15–16 June	5	25 June K	5	81-58930 ♂
1972	81-58936	LMA	Second	2–5 July	4	18–19 July	4	28 July K	4	none
1973	81-58936	LMA	First	2–5 June	4	18 June	4	28 June K	4	820-89211 ♂
1973	81-58936	LMA	Second	3–5 July	3	18 July	3	27 July K	3	820-89288 ♀
1974	830-20585	LMA	First	27–31 May	5	15–16 June K	5	25 June K	5	830-20530 ♀
										830-20532 ♀
1974	830-20585	LMA	Second	3–6 July	4	20 July K	4	30 July K	4	none
1975	830-20519	LMA	First	28 May–1 June K	5	13–14 June K	5	23 June K	5	860-40330 ♀
1976	830-20519	LMA	First	30 May–3 June K	5	16–17 June K	5	yg died K 22 June	0	—
Mean First Nesting				30 May–3 June	4.80	16–17 June	4.33	26 June	3.5	4 ♀, 2 ♂
Mean Second Nesting				3–5 July	3.67	19 July	3.67	28 July	3.67	

*The outcome of 1970 nest is unknown, but two young are assumed to have fledged.
K = known date; other dates are estimates.

exhibited by males and females will be discussed later.

Bruce Radabaugh (1966 and in litt.) banded 298 nestlings at Mack Lake, Oscoda County, from 1963 through 1973. Twenty-five of these were found during subsequent years for an overall return rate for both sexes of 8.4%.

Of the 446 banded fledged nestlings, 377 (84.5%) were from first broods and 69 (15.5%) were from second broods (Table 1). Forty warblers from first broods were recaptured in subsequent years yeilding a 10.6% return rate. Only one warbler (a female) from a second brood was subsequently recaptured, a 1.4% return rate.

Remating

Female 27 (80-57193), Male 30 (80-57192) and Male 39 (81-58854). Male 30 was captured on 27 June 1971 on the Artillery Range South, section 16. He was mated with Female 27. Their nest contained three warbler nestlings and one very large cowbird nestling. The cowbird escaped, but the three warbler nestlings were banded. In 1972 Male 30 mated with Female 81-58921 and their nest was located 165 m from his 1971 nest site. Although the five nestlings were very large when the nest was located, one was found dead on 20 June one meter from the nest. None of the other nestlings or their mother was ever seen again. In 1972 and 1973 Female 27 mated with Male 39. Her first 1972 nest produced five fledged nestlings from five eggs on 25 June, while her second 1972 nest yielded three fledged nestlings from four eggs on 31 July (Figure 42). In 1973 this pair nested 159 m north of their 1972 nests and only 3 m from the edge of the road. Five nestlings were removed by a predator from this nest on 1 July. In 1974 Male 39 was found .8 km to the north feeding a fledged cowbird on the Artillery Range North. During 1975 he mated with an unbanded female on the same territory on the Artillery Range North and five nestlings fledged on 28 June. He was not found again.

Mayfield (1960) lists five pairs of Kirtland's Warblers which mated on or very close to the same territory during two successive years. Some pairs also remated during a later year after a space of a year or more during which they were not located. Mayfield also lists seven pairs that could have re-mated a second year but did not. In the course of my field studies, I iden-tified 18 pairs which could have remated. Of these 18 pairs, 14 did remate. The average distance between the first and second year nesting sites of these 14 pairs was 92.2 m. For all 18 males the average distance between nest locations during successive years was 115 m (range, 38.1 m to 422.6 m). One pair definitely mated for three successive summers (1975–1977). Four of the original 18 pairs changed mates. These four males had nests their second summer at distances of 209 m, 165 m, 137 m, and 217 m from their first-year nests. The four females all nested on territories adjoining the ones

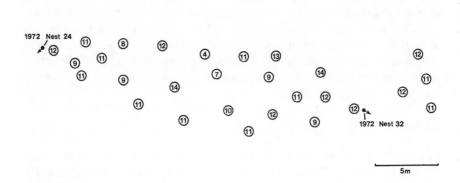

FIGURE 42.   Nest Locations of Female 27 and Male 39 in 1972 (Nests 24 and 32) on the Artillery Range South (Section 16, T27N, R2W).

occupied by their former mates. Distances between the first and second year nests of these females were 357 m, 247 m, 232 m, and 137 m. None of these pairs remated once they had separated.

Longevity of Adults

Forty-seven birds banded as nestlings were recaptured in subsequent years. Twenty-seven of these birds were males of which none was known to be alive at the beginning of the 1982 breeding season. Life histories of these males are summarized in Table 13 and in Figures 3, 4, and 5. The average age of these males when last seen can be used as a conservative estimate of the average age attained by male Kirtland's Warblers which survived to breed at least once. For all 27 males this average age was 4.0 ± 1.90 years (Table 35). This is only a rough approximation of the age attained by males which survive their first winter. Some males after breeding in one region may settle in later years outside the study regions and so remain undetected. Distances between the birthplaces of males and the territories they established in subsequent years are discussed in Chapter 7.

The life span of only one male is known precisely. This bird, banded on 2 July 1971 by Bruce Radabaugh when too young to fly, was killed flying into a picture window at Westwood, a suburb of Cincinnati, Ohio, on 27 September 1975. The bird was four years and three months of age when killed. It was banded at Mack Lake, Oscoda County, and had bred for four summers on Lovells Management Area, Crawford County.

Twenty females banded as nestlings returned to Michigan to breed at least once. None was found after the summer of 1978 (Tables 14 and 35). The average age of these females when last seen was 2.50 ± 1.85 years.

The survival spans of Kirtland's Warblers banded as adults (i.e. for birds that survived at least one year prior to banding) are minimum estimates since the age at banding is not known. Of 125 birds banded as adults, the minimum period of survival was 2.56 ± 1.93 years (Table 35). Since these estimates were made in late July and nearly 10 months elapsed between this time and the following spring when the birds could have been found again in Michigan, these birds may have lived about one-half year longer.

CHAPTER 13

BROWN-HEADED COWBIRD

History

The Brown-headed Cowbird has undoubtedly been the worst enemy of Kirtland's Warblers on the nesting grounds in this century. N. A. Wood and Frothingham (1905) reported the cowbird was common along the Au Sable valley in 1903. Strong (1919) found a nest in Crawford County on 31 May 1908 containing two cowbird eggs and two Kirtland's Warbler eggs. Edward Arnold (Mayfield 1962b) reported several warbler nests containing cowbird eggs around 1910. Walter Barrows (Mayfield 1962b) found a nest in Iosco County on 21 June 1920 which contained two warbler eggs and three cowbird eggs. Leopold (1924) reported a nest containing one warbler egg and one cowbird nestling on 20 June 1923 in Iosco County. Both Wood and Leopold expressed concern over excessive parasitism of Kirtland's Warblers by cowbirds. Mayfield (1960) reported that out of a group of 137 completed Kirtland's Warbler clutches, 75 contained one or more cowbird eggs (55%). He also reported that five more of the completed clutches were later parasitized. I found my first parasitized Kirtland's Warbler nest on 21 June 1932 near Red Oak, Oscoda County. The female warbler was incubating one warbler and two cowbird eggs.

Brown-headed Cowbirds generally arrive on the Kirtland's Warbler breeding grounds in late April or early May. They remain in small groups usually comprised of more males than females. Cowbirds continuously patrol the breeding grounds until mid-July when they move elsewhere. The females lay their eggs in clutches (Nice 1949) at the rate of one per day during the early morning (Hann 1941; Mayfield 1960; Nolan 1978). They usually remove one or all of the host eggs from the nest, but at times no eggs are removed. The cowbird lays its eggs from late May to mid-July. This is the same period that Kirtland's Warblers are nesting.

Cowbird eggs are larger than warbler eggs. The average measurement of 21 cowbird eggs found on the warbler nesting grounds was 21.7 mm × 17 mm and the average weight was 3.2 g. Cowbird eggs are nearly white in color and are sparingly covered with brown or blackish spots. They hatch in 11–12 days. Nestlings remain in the nest eight or nine days. Since the cowbird does not build its own nest or rear its own young, it lays its eggs in other birds' nests, particularly nests belonging to slightly smaller birds. Cowbirds depend on the host species to care for the eggs and nestlings. Kirtland's Warblers hatch the cowbird eggs and care for the nestlings as if they were their own until the fledglings are independent.

Kirtland's Warbler eggs require two or three more days of incubation than cowbird eggs. A nestling cowbird weighing 2 g when it hatches will weigh 10–13 g by the time any warbler eggs hatch. The newly hatched warbler which weighs 1.2–1.7 g does not stand a chance of survival unless it is hatched in a nest where the warbler eggs were laid before the cowbird eggs.

Parasitism of the Nest

Cowbirds lay their eggs very early in the morning. The exact time of day when cowbird eggs were laid was not known, but the day of laying was known in several instances. In 1971 at Nest 11 a cowbird egg was built into the bottom of a warbler nest so that it was completely covered. The egg must have been laid when the warbler was just beginning to build her nest. A nest found on 31 May 1972 contained only two deserted cowbird eggs. It was not known whether the warbler had laid any eggs in this nest. In 1938 at Nest 1 warbler eggs were laid on 5–8 June. A single cowbird egg appeared on the morning of 4 June. The warbler could have laid an egg that morning which may have been removed by the cowbird. Most unparasitized warbler nests contain five eggs, but only four warbler eggs were found in this nest.

In 1957 at Nest 4 there were three warbler eggs on 31 May and five warbler eggs by 2 June. On 11 June all the warbler eggs had disappeared and there were two cowbird eggs in their place. In 1957 at Nest 7 four Kirtland's Warbler eggs were laid on 5–8 June and cowbird eggs were laid on 7–8 June. On 8 June only one warbler egg remained and by 9 June all the warbler eggs had been removed. In 1970 at Nest 3 four warbler eggs were laid on 31 May–3 June. On 15 June one warbler egg had disappeared; on 16 June the second warbler egg disappeared; on 17 June a third warbler egg disappeared and one cowbird egg appeared; on 18 June the fourth warbler egg disappeared and the nest was deserted. On 22 June I placed two infertile Kirtland's Warbler eggs from another nest into this nest with the single cowbird egg. The following morning only the cowbird egg remained.

In 1970 at Nest 6 four Kirtland's Warbler eggs were laid on 19–23 June and a cowbird egg was laid on 20 June. The second warbler egg was still in the nest at 0830 hrs EST, but had disappeared by 1200 hrs EST on 20 June. On 21 June a third warbler egg was laid, but the first warbler egg had disappeared. On 22 June no new egg was observed and the female began incubating the eggs in the evening. On 23 June the female was incubating two warbler eggs (the third and fourth eggs laid) and one cowbird egg. I made a hole in the cowbird egg. On 7 July the female was brooding one small nestling who was the only survivor in this nest. In 1970 at Nest 13 the first warbler egg was laid during the early morning of 23 June. By 7 July the nest contained three warbler eggs and two small cowbirds which weighed 3.5 g and 2.1 g. On 9 July the first two of the three warbler eggs hatched and the cowbirds were removed. In 1971 at Nest 3 a cowbird egg appeared on 4 June. Warbler eggs appeared on 5–6 June, but were taken from the nest by a predator.

In 1974 at Nest 38 there was one warbler egg and one cowbird egg on 19 July. The cowbird egg hatched on 21 July. At 0900 hrs on 23 July the cowbird nestling lay alone in the bottom of the nest while the warbler nestling lay dead 3 cm in front of the nest. In all parasitized nests observed, no cowbird egg or nestling had disappeared except when removed by a predator or human. Indications are very strong that cowbirds differentiate between their own eggs and those of their warbler host and also between their own nestlings and warbler nestlings (Mayfield 1960).

Desertions

In 1933 at Nest 1 two cowbird eggs were removed. The warblers deserted this nest and their two eggs. I know of only four other cases in which the warbler deserted its nest. In 1957 at Nest 4 the five warbler eggs disappeared on 11 June. On this same day two cowbird eggs appeared and the nest was deserted. In 1967 Nest 6 was deserted when it contained only four cowbird eggs. In 1970 Nest 8 contained only two cowbird eggs and was deserted on 19 June. In 1972 Nest 5 was deserted in late May when it contained only two cowbird eggs. On two other occasions, the warblers did not desert nests that contained only four or three cowbird eggs, respectively. On a number of occasions nests containing only two cowbird eggs have been maintained by warblers.

On 24 June 1971 I removed two-, four- or five-day-old cowbirds from a Kirtland's Warbler nest and placed them in a Blue Jay nest containing four eggs. The Blue Jay raised the cowbird nestlings at the sacrifice of its own four eggs which never hatched. In another instance, two cowbird nestlings were placed in a Red-winged Blackbird nest and they were reared along with the blackbird nestlings.

Warbler eggs in parasitized nests often fail to hatch. This is probably due to the fact that the warblers stop incubating their own eggs adequately. Since the cowbird eggs hatch two or three days before the warbler eggs, both warblers begin feeding the cowbird nestlings. The warbler eggs are exposed, become chilled, and the embryos die as a result. Warbler eggs in parasitized nests frequently showed breaks in the surface. Such breaks were never found in eggs from unparasitized nests, thus it is likely that this damage was caused by adult cowbirds.

Sixty-eight parasitized Kirtland's Warbler nests contained 146 warbler eggs or 2.2 eggs per nest. Two hundred forty-one unparasitized nests contained 1,102 warbler eggs or 4.6 eggs per nest. The 68 parasitized nests should have contained a total of 313 eggs at that rate. Only one parasitized nest fledged both a cowbird (one) and warblers (two). Mayfield (1960) found that no warblers were fledged from parasitized nests which contained two or more cowbird nestlings. Four nests each contained one cowbird egg. In each instance this egg failed to hatch. Three, four, four, and two warblers, respectively, were fledged from these four nests. The nest which had the cowbird egg built into its bottom also produced two fledged warbler nestlings. In 1970 cowbird eggs were removed from three parasitized nests and six warbler nestlings were fledged (three, two, and one, respectively). A total of nine parasitized warbler nests produced 23 nestling warblers and only one cowbird. No warblers fledged from the other 59 parasitized nests. In contrast, 26 cowbird eggs hatched and could have fledged from 18 of these 59 nests. Thirty-one cowbird eggs in the remaining 41 parasitized nests were still viable at the time of my last visit. At least three of the parasitized warbler nests were destroyed by predators.

Amount of Parasitism

The 50 years during which I have studied Kirtland's Warblers can be divided into three definite periods. The first period extended from 1931 until the mid-1950s. During this period moderate parasitism of Kirtland's Warblers was observed (Table 22). Twenty-eight Kirtland's Warbler nests were studied. Three nests had incomplete clutches and seven nests were parasitized (25%). The 18 unparasitized nests contained 89 warbler eggs or 4.9 eggs per nest. The seven parasitized nests contained 14 warbler eggs (2.0 eggs per nest) and 12 cowbird eggs (1.7 eggs per nest). The second period extended from 1957 through 1971. In 1957 at Mack Lake, Oscoda County, 11 Kirtland's Warbler nests were observed. All were parasitized. These nests contained 39 warbler eggs early in the summer, but only 29 warbler eggs subsequently or 3.5 warbler eggs per nest at first sighting and 2.7 warbler eggs per nest later. These 11 nests also contained 19 cowbird eggs or 1.7 eggs per nest. From 1966 through 1971 no adult cowbirds were removed from the Artillery Range. Fifty-two Kirtland's Warbler nests were found of which 36 were parasitized (69.2%). The 36 parasitized nests contained 55 cowbird eggs (1.6 eggs per nest) and 68 warbler eggs (1.9 eggs per nest). During this period 42 pairs of warblers produced only 52 fledged warbler nestlings (0.81 fledged nestlings per nest or per pair for the summer). Thirty-six cowbird eggs and nestlings were also removed and the data indicate that this interference allowed 15–29 warbler nestlings to fledge which would otherwise not have survived. The third period extended from 1972 through 1977 and will be discussed in a later section of this chapter.

Reduction of Parasitism

Shake and Mattsson (1975: 48) reported, "As early as 1966 Cuthbert and Radabaugh realized that parasitism posed a threat to the warbler population and undertook a study to determine whether selective cowbird trapping and shooting could reduce parasitism of warbler nests. The results showed that parasitism was reduced from 65 to 21 percent."

When the 1971 census of singing male Kirtland's Warblers was published (Mayfield 1972a) only 201 males were recorded indicating a drastic decline in population from the 1961 count. A meeting of interested persons and representatives from conservation agencies and organizations was held in Ann Arbor on 30 October 1971 and the Kirtland's Warbler Advisory Committee was formed. The organizations involved were the Michigan Audubon Society, the Michigan Department of Natural Resources, the U.S. Fish and Wildlife Service, the U.S. Forest Service, the University of Michigan, the Detroit Audubon Society, and the Pontiac Audubon Society (Shake and Mattsson 1975). During the winter of 1972, I published the results of my six year (1966–1971) study of Kirtland's Warblers at the Artillery Range, Crawford County. This study showed how severe cowbird parasitism had become and how low the reproduction rate of the warblers had fallen.

The Kirtland's Warbler Advisory Committee recommended that several actions be taken to ensure the recovery of the species (Shake and Mattsson 1975). These recommendations included:

1. Encouraging state and federal agencies to manage more land for warbler nesting habitat through controlled burnings, selective cutting, and jack pine plantings.

2. Encouraging governmental agencies to acquire more lands suitable for warbler nesting.

3. Encouraging governmental agencies to limit public use of warbler nesting areas during the nesting season.

4. Conducting an annual census of the warbler population, especially singing males.

5. Implementation of extensive cowbird control program on major nesting areas.

Field work based on these recommendations began in May 1972 under the leadership of the U.S. Fish and Wildlife Service, the U.S. Forest Service, the Michigan Department of Natural Resources, and the Michigan, Detroit, and Pontiac Audubon Societies. Fifteen cowbird decoy traps were erected on seven of the major warbler nesting areas in Crawford, Oscoda, and Ogemaw Counties. These traps have been operated each year from 25 April to 15 July. About 12 cowbirds are placed in each trap as decoys. The traps are 4.9 m square, 1.8 m high, and have a 1.2 m square entrance in the center of the top. Sunflower seeds are placed on a board beneath this entrance. Captured cowbirds are asphyxiated with automobile exhaust which produced death in several seconds. The results of the trapping program for the years 1972 through 1977 are given in Table 42. By 1981, 40,000 adult cowbirds had been trapped.

After the U.S. Endangered Species Act of 1973 and the Michigan Endangered Species Act of 1974 were passed, the Kirtland's Warbler Recovery Team was formed. This team consisted of John Byelich, Chairman; G. W. Irvine, U.S. Forest Service; W. R. Jones and R. Radtke, U.S. Fish and Wildlife Service; H. Mayfield, Toledo, Ohio; N. I. Johnson, Michigan Department of Natural Resources. This team has met twice each year since its formation to establish methods to benefit Kirtland's Warbler.

From 1972 through 1977, under the supervision of the U.S. Fish and Wildlife Service, I studied the effect of cowbird trapping on the nesting success of Kirtland's Warblers (this was the third period of my field studies). Kirtland's Warbler eggs were observed in 230 nests. Eggs hatched in 190 nests (82.6%) and fledged from 160 nests (69.6%). Nine hundred seventy-one Kirtland's Warbler eggs were observed in these 230 nests of which 731 eggs hatched (75.3%) and 615 nestlings fledged (63.3%). The number of nestlings fledged per nest was 2.67. The 230 nests belonged to 198 pairs, thus the number of nestlings fledged per pair per year was 3.11 (Table 43). The success of nests located on naturally burned regions is compared to the success of nests located in man-made plantations (Table 44). One hundred twenty-three nests were found in naturally burned regions. Eggs hatched in 95 nests (88.8%) and nestlings fledged from 74 nests (69.2%). A total of 453 eggs was observed of which 351 eggs hatched (77.5%) and 286 nestlings fledged (63.1%). The success of both nests and eggs in each region was nearly identical.

Fourteen of these 230 nests were parasitized. The 216 unparasitized nests (containing 947 eggs) had an average clutch size of 4.4 eggs. Even with the inclusion of the parasitized nests (971 eggs) the average clutch size 4.2 eggs. During the first period, 1931–1955, 21 unparasitized nests contained 94 warbler eggs or an average clutch size of 4.5 eggs. Twenty-eight nests, both parasitized and unparasitized, had an average clutch size of 3.9 warbler eggs. During the second period, 1957–1971, 63 nests had an average clutch size

TABLE 42. Kirtland's Warbler Nesting Success After Removal of Brown-headed Cowbirds, 1966–1977.

Years	Cowbirds Removed	Kirtland's Warbler					
		Singing Male Count	No. of Pairs Studied	Nestlings Fledged per Nest	Nestlings Fledged per Pair During Year	Number and Per Cent of Parasitized Nests	
1966–1971	24 Eggs 18 Nestlings	201*	52	0.807	0.807	36 of 52	69.23
1972	2,200 Adults	200	26	2.72	3.35	2 of 32	6.25
1973	3,305 Adults	216	27	2.70	3.41	0 of 34	0.0
1974	4,075 Adults	167	54	2.87	3.35	6 of 63	9.52
1975	3,650 Adults	179	32	2.76	3.19	2 of 37	5.40
1976	4,299 Adults	200	30	2.70	2.97	2 of 33	6.06
1977	3,284 Adults	219	29	2.06	2.21	2 of 31	6.45

*1971 count
Numbers of adult cowbirds removed taken from Mattsson and DeCapita (1977: Table 4).
Singing male counts taken from Mayfield 1972, 1973a, 1973b, Ryel 1976a, 1976b, 1978b.

TABLE 43. Kirtland's Warbler Nesting Success in All Nests, 1972–1977.

Year	N Pairs	N Nests	No. with Hatching Eggs	No. with Fledging Young	No. of Eggs Laid	No. of Eggs Hatched	No. of Young Fledged	Number of Nestlings Fledged during Year	
								Per Pair	Per Nest
1972	26	32	26 (81.3%)	22 (68.8%)	135	106 (78.5%)	87 (64.4%)	3.35	2.72
1973	27	34	29 (85.3%)	23 (67.6%)	150	115 (76.7%)	92 (61.3%)	3.41	2.70
1974	36	42	34 (80.9%)	30 (71.4%)	174	126 (72.4%)	114 (65.5%)	3.17	2.71
1975	32	37	31 (83.8%)	26 (70.3%)	162	119 (73.6%)	102 (63.0%)	3.19	2.77
1976	30	33	27 (81.8%)	23 (69.7%)	134	104 (77.6%)	89 (66.4%)	2.97	2.70
1977	29	31	23 (74.3%)	19 (61.3%)	132	87 (65.9%)	64 (48.4%)	2.21	2.06
1974*	18	21	20 (95.2%)	17 (80.9%)	84	74 (88.1%)	67 (79.8%)	3.72	3.19
Total Per Cent	198	230	190 (82.6%)	160 (69.6%)	971	731 (75.3%)	615 (63.3%)	3.11	2.67

*This table and future tables include the 1974 nests found by Craig Orr (data used with his permission).

TABLE 44. Nesting Success of Kirtland's Warblers by Region, 1972–1977.

Years	Region	Number of KW Nests Found With KW & C Eggs	Number of KW Nests Where KW Eggs Hatched	Number of KW Nests Where KW Nestlings Fledged	Number of KW Eggs Observed	Number of KW Eggs Hatched	Number of KW Nestlings Fledged	Cowbird Parasitism Nests Parasitized	C Eggs/Young Laid	C Eggs/Young Hatched	C Eggs/Young Fledged
1972–76	ARS	55	39	32	246	162	128	2	4	2	1(1)
1973–77	ARN	22	14	14	94	57	55	2	2	1	1
1972–77	LMA	93	81	63	394	304	239	2	2	2	(1)
1972–75	PC	17	16	16	73	63	62	1	2	2	2
1976–77	KL	3	3	2	12	12	7	1	1	0	0
1976	NDRR	1	1	0	1	1	0	0	0	0	0
1974–77	ML	13	11	11	59	47	47	0	0	0	0
1974–77	MaL	14	14	11	51	48	41	3	4	4	(2)
1975–77	Damon	11	10	10	36	32	31	3	6	5	2 (3)
1977	Roscommon	1	1	1	5	5	5	0	0	0	0
Total		230	190	160	971	731	615	14	21	16 (17)	6 (13)

The numbers in parentheses indicate potential cowbird success, but cowbird eggs and nestlings were removed from most nests. Parasitism from 1972–1977 was 0.061%.

KW = Kirtland's Warbler   C = Cowbird

of 2.57 eggs or more than one egg less than during the first period. Sixteen unparasitized nests found during this second period contained 52 warbler eggs or 3.3 eggs per clutch. Cowbirds either removed eggs from both parasitized and unparasitized nests or created enough disturbance to cause female Kirtland's Warblers to lay fewer eggs. During the third period, 1972–1977, only 24 warbler eggs were found in 14 parasitized nests or 1.71 eggs per nest. These nests also contained 21 cowbird eggs or 1.5 eggs per nest. Cowbird eggs and nestlings were removed from all of these nests where possible, allowing at least 14 warblers to fledge ($\bar{x} = 1.0$).

Table 45 lists the contents of all parasitized Kirtland's Warbler nests that I observed from 1931 through 1977. The 68 nests studied contained 147 warbler eggs ($\bar{x} = 2.16$ eggs per nest) of which 55 eggs hatched (37.4%) and 42 nestlings fledged (28.6%). These same 68 nests contained 107 cowbird eggs ($\bar{x} = 1.57$ eggs per nest). Forty-four of the cowbird eggs were known to hatch and 25 young fledged. Without human interference, 55 cowbirds would have fledged (51.4%). If the 68 parasitized nests had contained a normal clutch of 4.38 warbler eggs, the total number of warbler eggs in these nests would have been 298. A fledging success rate of 63.3% for these 298 eggs would have produced 187 fledged nestlings instead of 42. This represents a loss of 145 or more Kirtland's Warblers. The actual nesting success was also improved by the removal of cowbird eggs and nestlings. These records graphically demonstrate the devastating decline in the warbler population directly attributable to cowbird parasitism.

Cowbird Parasitism of Other Species

Fifty-five other species of birds have been found on the habitat occupied by Kirtland's Warbler. Forty-five of these species have been found breeding there. Several hundred nests of these species have been found, but only seven nests were parasitized by cowbirds. Some of these species and the number of their nests observed are listed below:

Nashville Warbler (*Vermivora ruficapilla*). A nest found on 4 June 1971 contained two host eggs and one cowbird egg. At another nest, four nestlings fledged from five eggs on 19 June 1972. A third nest lost four eggs on 11 June 1979 and a fourth nest lost five nestlings to a predator on or about 15 June 1979. These nests are similar structurally to Kirtland's Warbler nests, but the eggs are smaller.

Yellow-rumped Warbler (*Dendroica coronata*). One nest found on 20 July 1932 contained four warbler nestlings and no cowbird nestlings.

Pine Warbler (*Dendroica pinus*). Two nests of this species have been found. The nest observed on 5 June 1938 contained one cowbird egg.

Prairie Warbler (*Dendroica discolor*). I found six nests of this species

TABLE 45. Contents of Parasitized Kirtland's Warbler Nests.

Years	Kirtland's Warbler				Brown-headed Cowbird		
	No. of Nests	No. of Eggs Observed	No. of Eggs Hatched	No. of Young Fledged (Probable)	No. of Eggs Observed	No. of Eggs Hatched	No. of Young Fledged (Possible)
1931–1955	7	14	2	2	12	3	3 (4)
1957	11	39	9	9	19	2	2 (5)
1966	6	1	0	0	9	6	6 (9)
1967	2	0	0	0	6	2	0 (2)
1968	1	4	0	0	1	0	0 (0)
1969	7	17	2	2	10	3	3 (8)
1970	11	30	16	9	16	8	4? (9)
1971	9	18	6	6	13	5	1 (6)
1972	2	1	0	0	4	2	1 (2)
1973	0						
1974	6	13	13	7	7	6	1 (4)
1975	2	3	3	3	4	3	2 (3)
1976	2	4	2	2	2	1	0
1977	2	3	2	2	4	3	2 (4)
Total	68	147	55 (37.4%)	42 (28.6%)	107	44 (41.1%)	25 (56) (23.4%) (52.4%)

2.16 Kirtland's Warbler eggs per parasitized nest.
1.57 Brown-headed Cowbird eggs per parasitized nest.

and Andrew J. Berger found an additional six nests. Two of these 12 nests were parasitized (one cowbird egg each).

Chestnut-sided Warbler (*Dendroica pensylvanica*). Although this bird does not nest in the jack pines, it does nest nearby in brushy country. A nest found at Lovells Management Area was not parasitized.

Western Palm Warbler (*Dendroica palmarum palmarum*). Two nests found on Kirtland's Warbler habitat were not parasitized, nor were nests found at Seney, Schoolcraft County.

Purple Finch (*Carpodacus purpureus*). One nest found on the Artillery Range South was not parasitized.

Rufous-sided Towhee (*Pipilo erythrophthalmus*). Several nests were found and none of them was parasitized.

Vesper Sparrow (*Pooecetes gramineus*). This is a very common species, but no nest has ever been found parasitized. Twenty-four nests were found.

"Slate-colored" or Northern Junco (*Junco hyemalis*). Four nests were found at the Artillery Range South and one was parasitized with two cowbird eggs.

Chipping Sparrow (*Spizella passerina*). I have observed 19 nests in warbler habitat of which two were parasitized (one cowbird egg each).

Clay-colored Sparrow (*Spizella pallida*). I have seen 40 nests of this species on or near warbler habitat. None of these nests were parasitized.

Field Sparrow (*Spizella pusilla*). Twelve nests of this species were found on warbler habitat. None of these nests were parasitized. Farther south in Calhoun County, the Field Sparrow was the cowbird's favorite host. Six hundred eighty-five Field Sparrow nests were found in Pennfield Township, Calhoun County, of which 26.6% (182 nests) were parasitized. Twenty-four other species were found nesting in this area, but only 4.3% of their nests were parasitized (12 out of 279 nests). The Field Sparrow is not a particularly good host for the cowbird since the sparrow's incubation period of 11 days is 1 day shorter than the cowbird's incubation period. The sparrow nestlings thus have a head start on the cowbird nestlings. The young sparrows are stronger and can claim more food from their parents than the young cowbirds can.

Lincoln's Sparrow (*Melospiza lincolnii*). A nest containing five eggs was found on the Artillery Range South on 15 June 1972. A second nest was found on the Artillery Range North on 31 May 1975 and a third nest was found on 4 June 1975 (four eggs each). A fourth nest was found on 30 May 1975 at Muskrat Lake. None of these nests was parasitized.

Song Sparrow (*Melospiza melodia*). Two nests have been found on the Artillery Range North. Neither nest was parasitized.

Farther south in Muskegon County and Calhoun County, three *Empidonax* flycatchers were occasionally parasitized:

Acadian Flycatcher (*Empidonax virescens*). One hundred twenty-one nests belonging to this species were found. Twenty-five of these nests were parasitized (20.7%).

Alder Flycatcher (*Empidonax alnorum*). Ninety-four nests of this species were found of which five were parasitized (5.32%).

Least Flycatcher (*Empidonax minimus*). Fifty-four nests of this species were found of which five were parasitized (9.3%). All three of these flycatchers have incubation periods of 13–15 days, similar to that of Kirtland's Warbler.

These data demonstrate that the cowbird is clearly selective about the species of bird it chooses to parasitize in each habitat.

Advantages to the Cowbird in Parasitizing Kirtland's Warbler Nests

It is not known why a large number of Brown-headed Cowbirds have concentrated on the jack pine plains in the northern part of Michigan's Lower Peninsula. They cannot all have been reared in this area, but their areas of origin are not known with any certainty. They have come to depend upon the Kirtland's Warbler as their primary host for the following reasons:

1. Cowbirds normally perch on tall stubs where they can watch Kirtland's Warblers building their nests. The cowbird has unlimited time for observation. Kirtland's Warblers ignore the cowbirds and their movements unless they come close to the warbler's nest. Female cowbirds lay their eggs so early in the morning that the warblers are unaware that their nest has been approached. An additional egg or eggs simply appear.

2. A Kirtland's Warbler will not desert a nest containing one to four warbler eggs, even if there are as many as three cowbird eggs parasitizing it.

3. Kirtland's Warbler accepts the cowbird eggs. Only once did I find a cowbird egg built into the structure of a warbler nest and it was probably laid before the nest was completed.

4. Cowbird eggs are larger than host eggs and the newly hatched cowbird nestling is larger than the warbler nestlings.

5. Cowbird eggs have an 11–12 day incubation period whereas Kirtland's Warbler eggs require 13–15 days for incubation. Consequently, the 1.2–1.4 g newly hatched warbler must compete with a nest mate frequently weighing 13 g or more.

6. Cowbirds lay their eggs at the same time the warblers do.

7. Cowbirds can remove eggs from warbler nests without the host

deserting the nest. At times the cowbirds do not remove any warbler eggs. At other times they may remove the entire host clutch, leaving only cowbird eggs.

8. Kirtland's Warblers lose fewer nests to predation than many other species.

9. Kirtland's Warblers are very attentive to both the eggs and the nestlings in their nests whether they are their own or those of the cowbird.

10. Nestlings of both species can be fed on local insect food.

11. Kirtland's Warblers care for fledged cowbirds as diligently as their own until they become independent.

Summary

Mayfield (1960) graphically summarized the havoc produced by cowbird parasitism of Kirtland's Warbler nests. My own observations produced similar conclusions. The cowbird is apparently a recent invader of the Kirtland Warbler habitat. My data show that cowbirds were less common during the period 1931–1955 than during the period 1957–1971. The cowbird observes all other birds during the nesting season and selects its host species. In the jack pine habitat, I found 93% of all cowbird eggs in Kirtland's Warbler nests and only 7% in the nests of all other species combined. The cowbird lays its eggs very early in the morning, normally during the same five days the female warbler is laying. Occasionally, the cowbird will lay an egg before the first warbler egg is laid. At times more than one cowbird will utilize the same warbler nest. This is known because occasionally more than one cowbird egg will appear on a given day. Up to four cowbird eggs are commonly laid in a warbler nest.

The cowbird also removes eggs and in rare cases nestlings of the Kirtland's Warbler. Unparasitized warbler clutches normally contain three to six eggs ($\bar{x} = 4.38$ eggs), while parasitized nests contain an average of 2.16 warbler eggs per nest. On many occasions warbler eggs were damaged, apparently by cowbird intervention. My field studies record 68 parasitized warbler nests which contained a total of 107 cowbird eggs ($\bar{x} = 1.57$ cowbird eggs per nest). Mayfield found an average of 1.67 cowbird eggs per parasitized warbler nest. Only 42 warblers fledged from the 68 parasitized nests ($\bar{x} = 0.62$ fledglings per nest) compared to an average of 2.67 fledglings per nest from 230 parasitized and unparasitized nests (Table 42).

The cowbird lays a larger egg (3.2–3.4 g) than Kirtland's Warbler does and the incubation period of the cowbird eggs is shorter. Since the cowbird nestling hatches two days before the warbler, it can weight as much as 13 g when the 1.2 g warbler nestling arrives. If a nest contains two cowbird nestlings (hatching a day apart but both before the warblers), any nestling warblers that may subsequently hatch do not stand a chance for survival. The chances of a nestling warbler surviving in competition with even a single cowbird nestling are slim. Any species, such as Kirtland's Warbler, Acadian Flycatcher, or Alder Flycatcher, with an incubation period of 14–15 days, stands little chance for survival when competing with the cowbird. Birds, such as Chipping Sparrows or Field Sparrows, having shorter incubation periods of 11–12 days, are much less vulnerable. Both the cowbird and the warbler nestlings remain in the nest for about nine days, thus the cowbird nestling often fledges two days before the warbler nestlings. If the cowbird egg is laid after the warbler egg, the warbler nestlings have a slight advantage. However, many of the warbler eggs are still lost due to cowbird interference.

The benefit of the removal of adult cowbirds from Kirtland's Warbler habitat has been well documented. The amount of parasitism during the years 1931–1955 equalled 25% of the nests studied. The period from 1957 through 1971 saw the incidence of parasitism rise to 74.6% of the nests studied. After adult cowbirds were removed from the warbler habitat (1972–1977), only 14 of 230 nests were parasitized (6.1%). Unparasitized nests during the years 1931–1955 had an average of 4.9 warbler eggs per nest (18 nests), while the average fell to 3.3 warbler eggs per nest (16 nests) during the years 1957–1971. Between 1972 and 1977 the average rose to 4.6 warbler eggs per nest (207 nests). During the years 1966–1971 only 0.81 warbler nestlings fledged per nest. This number increased to 2.67 fledged nestlings per nest after cowbird removal.

These data (Tables 42 and 43) indicate that cowbird control has substantially increased the nesting success of Kirtland's Warblers. The customary method of calculating nesting success employed above is suitable for comparing relative numbers of warblers produced per pair before and after cowbird control, but it may be misleading to interpret these figures as indicators of the actual number of young produced per pair, since this traditional method of calculating nesting success often underestimates nest losses (Mayfield 1960). Thus, Mayfield's method of calculating nesting success is also used. The results of these calculations are reported in Chapter 14. However, since most of the adults and nestlings which I studied were banded, I was able to follow nesting success more closely than is usually the case. I probably underestimated nest losses only rarely.

CHAPTER 14

FACTORS INFLUENCING NESTING SUCCESS OF KIRTLAND'S WARBLER

Mark Bergland

Kirtland's Warbler (*Dendroica kirtlandii*) is particularly susceptible to brood parasitism by the Brown-headed Cowbird (*Molothrus ater*) and cowbird parasitism has been considered to be a major factor reducing the nesting success of this species (Mayfield 1960, 1977; Walkinshaw 1972; Walkinshaw and Faust 1974; and others). Statistical analyses by Anderson and Storer (1976) of data collected through the 1975 breeding season by Dr. L. H. Walkinshaw and other investigators revealed that cowbird control significantly increased nesting success of Kirtland's Warblers. Anderson and Storer (1976) also examined additional factors thought to be important to Kirtland's Warbler nesting success and presented management recommendations based on results of these analyses.

Cowbird control has apparently arrested the alarming decline in numbers of Kirtland's Warblers which occurred during recent years (Table 2), but the population remains at a dangerously low level and it is necessary to identify factors currently influencing nesting success of this species. The purpose of this chapter is twofold: (1) To examine nesting success of Kirtland's Warbler since the initiation of cowbird control using Mayfield's (1960,1975) method, which is based on determination of nest losses per unit of exposure of eggs and young to mortality factors. (2) To combine data collected by Dr. L. H. Walkinshaw during the 1976 and 1977 breeding seasons with the data set originally compiled by Anderson and Storer (1976), and to reexamine factors influencing nesting success by statistical analysis of this updated data set.

Nesting Success Calculated from Units of Exposure

The customary method of calculating nesting success is often unsatisfactory as an estimate of actual production of young, since it frequently underestimates nest losses and overstates success (Mayfield 1960:188; 1975). At current levels of control, cowbird parasitism is no longer an important source of mortality to Kirtland's Warbler eggs and young, but other factors such as predation could be important. Thus, it is necessary to use an unbiased estimator of nesting success when evaluating survival of eggs and young in the absence of cowbirds. Mayfield (1960, 1975) has developed such an estimator, which I used to calculate nesting success of Kirtland's Warblers from 1972 through 1977. Unless otherwise indicated, all references to Mayfield refer to his 1960 publication.

Numbers of nests lost to predation and desertion are presented in Table 46. All data used in this section were collected by Dr. L. H. Walkinshaw and are used with his permission. It is apparent from Table 46 that losses due to predation are considerably more common than losses due to desertion, especially during the nestling period. Nests lost per nest-day during the incubation and nestling periods (Table 46) are slightly greater than comparable losses reported by Mayfield for unparasitized nests (0.040 and 0.019 nests lost per nest-day, respectively).

Numbers of eggs lost per egg-day of observation from nests that otherwise survived the incubation period and numbers of nestlings lost per nestling-day from nests that otherwise survived the nestling period, are presented in Table 47. As can be seen from this table, the probability that an individual egg or nestling survived in a persisting nest was relatively high, meaning that most losses involved entire clutches or broods. This is in agreement with comparable results presented by Mayfield.

Using information from Tables 46 and 47, probabilities of survival of eggs and nestlings during the incubation and nestling periods are calculated in Table 48. An incubation period of 14 days and a nestling period of nine days were assumed for these calculations.

To calculate nesting success, it was also necessary to know the probability that an individual egg would hatch. One hundred thirty-seven nestlings were produced from 149 eggs present immediately before hatching; thus the hatching

TABLE 46.   Success of Kirtland's Warbler Nests During the Incubation and Nestling Periods.

Period	Nests	Nest-days	Nests Deserted	Nests Destroyed	Nests Lost	Nests Lost Per Nest-Day
Incubation	85	675	9	26	35	0.052
Nestling	133	780	1	19	20	0.026
Totals		1,455	10	45	55	0.038

Note: This table follows Mayfield's (1960) format.

TABLE 47. Success of Individual Eggs and Nestlings in Persisting
          Nests, 1972–1977.

Period	Nests	Egg-Days/ Nestling-Days	Eggs Lost/Nestlings Lost	Losses per Egg Day/Nestling Day
Incubation	85	2,831.5	2	0.001
Nestling	133	2,893.5	8	0.003

rate was 0.919. Nesting success was then calculated by multiplying the probability that an egg survived the incubation period (0.470) by the hatching rate (0.919) and multiplying the resulting product by the probability that a nestling survives the nestling period (0.772). Nesting success calculated from this procedure is 0.333, which is the probability that a Kirtland's Warbler egg will produce a nestling which successfully fledges. This value is considerably below the value calculated using the customary procedure (0.633), suggesting that losses due to predation are relatively high. Nest losses varied between years, so it is necessary to look at the long-term average rather than individual years when evaluating the importance of predation as a mortality factor.

Green (1977) has suggested that Mayfield's method may underestimate nesting success if certain nests are more vulnerable to predation than others. Green felt that this bias "will only be significant if risks are high and quite different from nest to nest." Nest vulnerability is a factor which is very difficult to quantify, however, and I have not attempted to classify nests according to this criterion. Dow (1978) stated that Green's modification of Mayfield's method should be used "when nests can be separated on any basis," such as habitat differences and differences in the age of breeding adults (and the commonness of certain predators-L.H.W.). For several rea-

TABLE 48. Probabilities of Survival of Eggs and Nestlings During the
          Incubation and Nestling Periods, 1972–1977.

Period	Probability that Nest Survives Incubation/Nestling Period		Probability of Survival of Eggs/Nestlings in Persisting Nests		Survival Rate
Incubation	$(0.948)^{14}$	×	$(0.999)^{14}$	=	0.470
Nestling	$(0.974)^{9}$	×	$(0.997)^{9}$	=	0.772

Note: Right sides of equations do not exactly equal left sides because probability values have been rounded off.

sons, I feel that it is not necessary to separate Kirtland's Warbler nests into these types of categories. Kirtland's Warbler has fairly rigid habitat requirements and nesting success in different regions is fairly uniform, as will be discussed. Walkinshaw's data (Table 29) suggest that young females are probably as successful as older females at raising offspring (see also Anderson and Storer 1976: Table 6). Other factors, such as time of year, could influence nest vulnerability of Kirtland's Warblers and thus, bias the estimate of nesting success presented in this chapter. Nevertheless, I believe that Mayfield's method is particularly applicable to this species. It gives a much more accurate estimate of nesting success than the conventional procedure, which does not correct for undetected nests lost early in the nesting cycle.

Yearly Production Per Pair

Mayfield concluded through a theoretical argument that 100 pairs of adult Kirtland's Warblers will attempt roughly 150 nestings per breeding season, allowing for renest attempts after destruction or desertion of previous nests. In his calculations Mayfield ignored attempts at raising second broods after successfully rearing first broods, since few instances of this behavior were known prior to 1960. Since that time Walkinshaw has discovered that this type of behavior is more common than previously thought. However, the rate of return of nestlings from second broods is very low and second nestings probably contribute relatively little to future generations. Thus, this type of production is ignored in the following discussion.

Using Mayfield's formulae, I attempted to estimate the number of nests started per breeding season by a pair of adult Kirtland's Warblers. For several reasons, however, I felt that a separate calculation of the number of nests started per pair per year was not justified by the precision of the data. Therefore, I will use Mayfield's estimate of 150 nests started by 100 pairs of adult warblers as a rough approximation of the actual number of nests started by 100 pairs of adults each year from 1972 through 1977. As Mayfield noted, this number may be unrealistically high, since it assumes that all nests lost within a certain period of time are replaced.

Walkinshaw reported that the average clutch size of Kirtland's Warbler since the initiation of cowbird control is 4.43 eggs per clutch, including parasitized nests. Multiplying 4.43 eggs per clutch times the probability that an egg will fledge (0.333) gives an estimated production of 1.48 fledglings per nesting attempt, a figure identical with that calculated by Mayfield for Kirtland's Warbler production in the absence of cowbirds. The closeness of these results is due to chance, since the component parts of Mayfield's calculations are different than mine, but multiplied together give the same product. That is, 4.63 eggs per clutch times 0.32 fledglings per egg equals 1.48 nestlings fledged per nesting attempt.

Using Mayfield's estimate of 1.5 nests started per pair per year and assuming that 1.48 fledglings are produced per nesting attempt, 100 adults would produce about 110 young per breeding season. Because the component parts are identical, this is the same figure reported by Mayfield for yearly production per pair assuming no interference by cowbirds.

Adult Survival

Mayfield estimated that about 60% of adult Kirtland's Warblers survived from one year to the next and that the life expectancy of an adult was about two years. Since then, Walkinshaw has gathered considerably more data on survival of adult Kirtland's Warblers, as he reported in Table 35. Survival of 172 adult birds from 1972 through 1977 was a minimum of 2.39 ± 1.76 years and the true figure could be considerably higher, since the known survival of 27 adult males banded as nestlings was 4.00 ± 1.90 years. Two of these birds were still alive at the end of the 1981 breeding season.

I have used information in Table 35 to estimate the percentage of adult warblers surviving from one year to the next. These percentages are given in Table 49 and were calculated by determining the numbers of banded birds in each category present the following year. Percentages given in Table 49 are minimum estimates of adult survival per year, since the method assumes that birds banded as adults were one year of age at the time of banding and that any banded adult not discovered the following year perished in the interim. Both of these assumptions are untrue, but Table 49 can be used to obtain a rough estimate of overall adult survival.

Estimates of female survival given in Table 49 are probably low, since females are less likely to be detected on the breeding grounds, as both Walkinshaw and Mayfield pointed out. Therefore, I believe that the true survival rate for females is close to the survival rates for adult males. It is difficult, however, to compare survival rates of males and females, since females may be more susceptible to predation while incubating or brooding and males may be more susceptible to predation while singing from exposed perches. Nevertheless, the actual survival rate of adult Kirtland's Warblers of both sexes may be above 65%.

Mayfield (1960) estimated that survival of Kirtland's Warblers during their first year of life would have to approach 36% in order to maintain a stable population, assuming that no nests are parasitized by cowbirds. Applying Mayfield's methodology to data collected by Walkinshaw from 1972 through 1977 gives the following estimate of first-year survival needed to maintain a stable population. As previously discussed 100 adult warblers produce roughly 110 young per year. If adult survival is currently 65%–70% per year, survival of young warblers during their first year would have to be 27%–32% (30/110 and 35/110 respectively) to maintain a stable population. Although this hypothetical rate of survival appears to be 'reasonably'

TABLE 49.   Percentages of Adult Warblers Surviving Each Year,
1972–1977.

Age When Banded	Males		Females	
	N	% Surviving Each Year	N	% Surviving Each Year
Adults	63	61.9	62	41.3
Nestlings	27	73.6	20	57.5
Combined	90	66.1	82	45.8

low, it is still greater than comparable survival rates of other small passerines during their first year of life, as Mayfield has indicated.

These results serve to reinforce Walkinshaw's argument that predation is an important source of mortality reducing nesting success of Kirtland's Warbler. Although cowbird control has been and still is an essential part of the management plan for this species, it is clear that activities of Blue Jays (*Cyanocitta cristata*) and other predators in nesting regions should be closely monitored. Selective removal of confirmed predators from the vicinity of nest sites may greatly increase nesting success of Kirtland's Warbler while minimizing disturbance to the population of native predators.

Other Factors Influencing Nesting Success

Anderson and Storer (1976) identified several factors which apparently have influenced nesting success of Kirtland's Warblers. In addition to the influence of cowbird parasitism on nesting success, they found that nesting success was significantly greater (1) when large trees and snags were removed from breeding grounds and (2) in flat compared to hilly terrain. Other factors were examined including mean stand height, colony age, age of breeding females, ground cover density, nest concealment, and number of researcher visits, but no significant effects on nesting success were apparent when these factors were analyzed.

Data analyses reported in Anderson and Storer (1976) involved data collected through 1975. Since that time, Dr. Lawrence H. Walkinshaw has collected additional data on Kirtland's Warbler breeding biology, which I added to the original data set on file at the University of Michigan Museum of Zoology. I was particularly interested in examining possible interactions among various factors thought to influence nesting success of Kirtland's Warblers.

Statistical Techniques

I used multi-way analysis of variance to examine the relative influence of five factors on nesting success: (1) presence or absence of large trees and snags, (2) topography (hilly versus flat terrain), (3) habitat treatment (planting of jack pines versus natural regeneration of jack pines through controlled burning), (4) stand height, and (5) presence or absence of cowbird control. Nesting success was considered to be the dependent variable in these models and was defined as the number of Kirtland's Warblers which fledged per nest. Number of Kirtland's Warbler eggs laid per nest and number of eggs which hatched per nest were also used as dependent variables in the multi-way ANOVA models.

Differences between marginal and cell means of the ANOVA models were tested by applying the Scheffé multiple comparison procedure. An alpha level of 0.05 was selected for all statistical tests except for the Sheffé procedure, where an alpha level of 0.10 was chosen because of the conservative nature of this test (Neter and Wasserman 1974).

When assumptions of the parametric models were not met, nonparametric procedures were employed, including the Kruskal-Wallis rank-sum test and the Wilcoxon matched-pair rank-sum test. This latter procedure was used to compare ages of stands selected for breeding by male warblers.

All statistical analyses were performed at the University of Michigan Computing Center. MIDAS, a library of statistical routines developed at the University of Michigan, was used to stratify the data, perform all analyses involving single-factor models, and examine the assumptions of these models. Multi-factor ANOVA models were analyzed using the computer program BMDX64.

Anderson and Storer (1976) provide a description of the methods used to compile the original data set, which consisted of data collected by Bruce E. Radabaugh, Lawrence H. Walkinshaw, Harold F. Mayfield, Josselyn Van Tyne, Warren R. Faust, and Craig D. Orr.

Results

Three factors were examined in the first ANOVA model: presence/absence of cowbird control, topography, and presence/absence of large trees and snags. Results of this analysis are summarized in Tables 50–52 and interactions among the factors are plotted in Figures 43 and 44.

The top three illustrations in Figure 43 represent the interaction between topography and presence/absence of large trees and snags, temporarily ignoring presence/absence of cowbird control as a factor in the model. If only this interaction is considered, it appears that snags have no influence on the numbers of Kirtland's Warblers fledged per nest in hilly terrain, but that nesting success is higher in flat terrain when snags are absent. One possible explanation is that cowbirds or predators could use either snags or hills as vantage points while searching for nests (Anderson and Storer 1976). Consequently, nesting success might be higher when neither snags nor hills are present in nesting habitat.

TABLE 50. Three-Way Analysis of Variance Model Using Number of Kirtland's Warblers Fledged per Nest as the Dependent Variable (1972–1977 not using Craig Orr's data).

Factor	Level	N	KW Fledged per Nest	Standard Error
Large Trees	Present	235	1.94	2.02
and Snags	Absent	100	2.47	2.03
Topography	Hilly	111	1.88	2.04
	Flat	224	2.21	2.03
Cowbird	Yes	224	2.55	2.04
Control	No	111	1.20	1.73

Analysis of Variance Table

Source	Degrees of Freedom	F-Statistic	Significant/Not Significant
Large Trees and Snags	1	1.24	NS
Topography	1	6.12	S
Cowbird Control	1	8.89	S
Snags × Topography	1	6.00	S
Topography × Cowbird Control	1	5.56	S
Snags × Cowbird Control	1	3.21	NS
Snags × Topography × Cowbird Control	1	0.65	NS
Error	327		

The interaction between presence/absence of cowbird control and topography (ignoring presence/absence of snags) is illustrated in the middle portion of Figure 43 and the interaction between presence/absence of cowbird control and presence/absence of snags (ignoring topography) is illustrated in the bottom portion of Figure 43. Before cowbirds were controlled, nesting success was apparently lower in hilly terrain compared to flat terrain and nesting success was also lower when large trees and snags were present in nesting regions.

Several trends are apparent when considering the relative influences of all three factors on nesting success:

1) Nesting success was relatively high in flat terrain when large trees and snags were not present, even in the absence of cowbird control. However, since only five nests fell into this category, the sample size is too small to make a valid statistical inference.

TABLE 51.   Three-Way Analysis of Variance Model Using Number of Kirtland's Warbler Eggs Laid per Nest as the Dependent Variable (1972–1977 not using Craig Orr's data).

Factor	Level	N	KW Eggs per Nest	Standard Error
Large Trees	Present	262	4.03	1.24
and Snags	Absent	85	4.45	0.93
Topography	Hilly	122	3.94	1.27
	Flat	225	4.24	1.13
Cowbird	Yes	193	4.60	0.80
Control	No	154	3.55	1.33

Analysis of Variance Table

Source	Degrees of Freedom	F-Statistic	Significant/Not Significant
Large Trees and Snags	1	2.16	NS
Topography	1	9.41	S
Cowbird Control	1	16.8	S
Snags × Topography	1	4.57	S
Topography × Cowbird Control	1	4.94	S
Snags × Cowbird Control	1	5.84	S
Snags × Topography × Cowbird Control	1	3.58	NS
Error	339		

2)   There appeared to be no effect of large trees and snags on nesting success in hilly terrain. However, since only six nests were located in hilly terrain without large trees and snags before the initiation of cowbird control, the sample size is too small to compare this cell mean with other cell means.

3)   When large trees and snags were present, nesting success was significantly higher after cowbirds were removed, regardless of topography. Using sample sizes given on the bottom portion of Figure 44 as points of reference, cell mean '39' was significantly higher than cell mean '37', and cell mean '96' was significantly higher than cell mean '63' (p < 0.10).

4)   The relative influence of topography on nesting success was evaluated by comparing cell mean '29' with cell mean '60', cell mean '39' with cell mean '96', and cell mean '37' with cell mean '63'. None of these differences was significant, suggesting (a) that cow-

TABLE 52.   Three-Way Analysis of Variance Model Using Number of Kirtland's Warbler Eggs Hatched per Nest as the Dependent Variable.

Factor	Level	N	KW Hatched Per Nest	Standard Error
Large Trees	Present	269	2.48	1.99
and Snags	Absent	97	2.99	1.94
Topography	Hilly	125	2.46	1.99
	Flat	241	2.70	1.99
Cowbird	Yes	216	3.06	1.94
Control	No	150	1.97	1.89

Analysis of Variance Table

Source	Degrees of Freedom	F-Statistic	Significant/Not
Large Trees and Snags	1	0.75	NS
Topography	1	4.41	S
Cowbird Control	1	7.38	S
Snags × Topography	1	6.28	S
Topography × Cowbird Control	1	6.14	S
Snags × Cowbird Control	1	3.37	NS
Snags × Topography × Cowbird Control	1	0.26	NS
Error	358		

bird control was equally effective in flat and hilly terrain and (b) that nesting success was about the same in flat and hilly terrain when snags were present, before cowbirds were removed from Kirtland's Warbler habitat.

Although interactions among the three factors used in the above model are complex, several management recommendations are apparent from these analyses. Cowbird control effectively increases nesting success of Kirtland's Warbler and this practice should be continued. If possible, new breeding areas should be established in flat regions free of large trees and snags, as Anderson and Storer (1976) originally suggested. This is especially important considering the high mortality rate of eggs and nestlings which is occurring in the absence of cowbirds. Blue Jays and other predators may locate warbler nests more easily if elevated vantage points are readily available.

The purpose of the second ANOVA model was to compare nesting success of Kirtland's Warblers in plantations with nesting success in burned

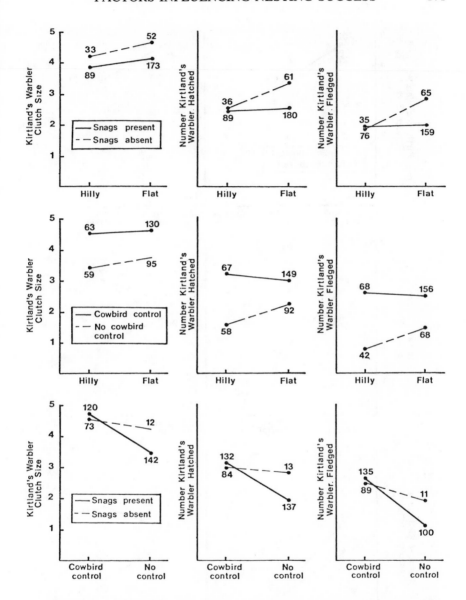

FIGURE 43. First-Order Interactions for the Three-Way ANOVA Model, Run Separately for Three Dependent Variables.

regions, before and after cowbird control. Results are summarized in Tables 53–55 and the interaction between habitat treatment and presence/absence of cowbird control is plotted in Figure 45.

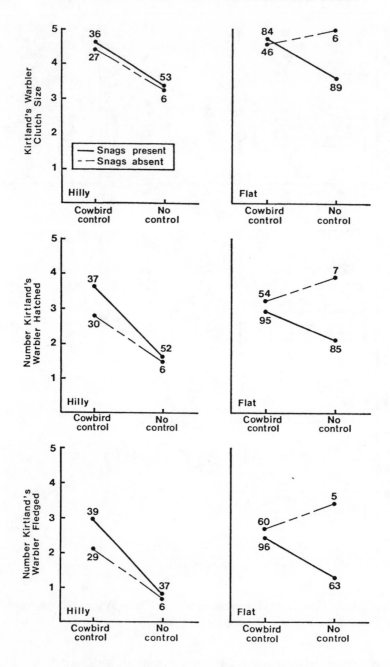

FIGURE 44.   Second-Order Interaction for the Three-Way ANOVA Model, Run Separately for Three Different Variables.

TABLE 53.   Two-Way Analysis of Variance Model Using Number of
Kirtland's Warblers Fledged per Nest as the Dependent
Variable.

Factor	Level	N	KW Fledged Per Nest	Standard Error
Treatment	Burning	117	1.91	2.00
	Planting	89	2.65	2.00
Cowbird	Yes	151	2.54	2.04
Control	No	55	1.40	1.77

Analysis of Variance Table

Source	Degrees of Freedom	F-Statistic	Significant/Not Significant
Treatment	1	10.3	S
Cowbird Control	1	2.89	NS
Treatment × Cowbird Control	1	8.34	S
Error	202		

Note: Only nests in flat terrain were included in this analysis.

TABLE 54.   Two-Way Analysis of Variance Model Using Number of
Kirtland's Warbler Eggs Laid per Nest as the Dependent
Variable.

Factor	Level	N	KW Eggs Per Nest	Standard Error
Treatment	Burning	128	4.06	1.25
	Planting	79	4.47	0.89
Cowbird	Yes	131	4.61	0.75
Control	No	76	3.54	1.36

Analysis of Variance Table

Source	Degrees of Freedom	F-Statistic	Significant/Not Significant
Treatment	1	8.09	S
Cowbird Control	1	28.2	S
Treatment × Cowbird Control	1	14.8	S
Error	203		

Note: Only nests in flat terrain were included in this analysis.

TABLE 55. Two-Way Analysis of Variance Model Using Number of Kirtland's Warbler Eggs Hatched per Nest as the Dependent Variable.

Factor	Level	N	KW Hatched Per Nest	Standard Error
Treatment	Burning	134	2.42	2.02
	Planting	86	3.19	1.84
Cowbird	Yes	145	3.00	1.97
Control	No	75	2.17	1.91

Analysis of Variance Table

Source	Degree of Freedom	F-Statistic	Significant/Not Significant
Treatment	1	9.75	S
Cowbird Control	1	1.73	NS
Treatment × Cowbird Control	1	5.72	S
Error	216		

Note: Only nests in flat terrain were included in this analysis.

When only nests located in flat terrain were considered, nesting success was higher in plantations compared to burned regions. However, this trend was only apparent before cowbirds were removed from Kirtland's Warbler habitat (bottom portion of Figure 45). Again using sample sizes on the figure as points of reference, cell mean '13' was significantly larger than cell mean '42' ($p < 0.05$). There was no difference between cell means '75' and '76' ($p > 0.10$), suggesting that nesting success was about the same in plantations and burnings after the initiation of cowbird control. Similar results were obtained when the analysis was rerun using data from nests located in flat, hilly and unknown terrain pooled together (top portion of Figure 45).

Topography could not be included as a factor in the preceding model because plantations were located almost exclusively in flat terrain. Thus, it is unclear whether increased nesting success in plantations was due to some characteristic of the plantations themselves or whether it was due to some characteristic related to topography. Perhaps the warblers were more successful in plantations prior to cowbird control because these areas had fewer large trees and snags than burned areas. The number of nests falling within this category was fairly small (Figure 45), because plantations were not as common as burned regions prior to the initiation of cowbird control. Thus, these results should be interpreted with caution. In addition, nesting success was defined in this model as the number of Kirtland's Warblers fledged per nest and this measure says nothing about the total productivity of plantations versus burned regions. That is, warblers may prefer one type of habitat over another if both are equally available and total productivity in the preferred habitat may be relatively high even though nesting success per pair is relatively low. More information is needed on the preference of warblers for

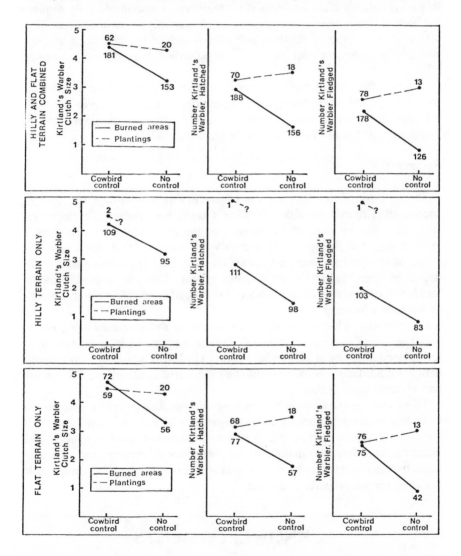

FIGURE 45.   Interaction Between Habitat Treatment and Presence/Absence of Cowbird Control for the Two-Way ANOVA Model, Run Separately for Three Different Dependent Variables.

habitat created by planting compared to habitat created by natural regeneration following forest fires.

Several multi-way ANOVA models were constructed using stand height as a factor in conjunction with various combinations of previously mentioned factors. There was some evidence that the warblers were more successful in younger stands after cowbirds were removed, especially in hilly terrain, but these differences were not significant. Apparently stand height had little effect on the number of Kirtland's Warblers fledged per nest, a conclusion which is in agreement with earlier results published by Anderson and Storer (1976).

Several other factors were also examined in relation to nesting success, including ground cover density, nest concealment, and distance to the nearest large tree or snag. Results were basically the same as those reported by Anderson and Storer (1976) for the original data set.

Summary

The purpose of this chapter was to identify factors influencing nesting success of Kirtland's Warbler. Nesting success has dramatically improved since the initiation of cowbird control, but the probability that a Kirtland's Warbler egg will fledge is still relatively low (0.33). Predation is now the single most important mortality factor on the breeding grounds and the activities of Blue Jays and other potential predators should be closely monitored. Selective removal of predators may greatly increase nesting success of Kirtland's Warbler.

Other factors influencing nesting successs were also examined using multi-way analysis of variance techniques. Results supported earlier management recommendations by Anderson and Storer (1976). If possible, new nesting habitat for Kirtland's Warbler should be established in extensive, flat regions free of large trees and snags.

There was some evidence that nesting success was higher in plantations compared to burned regions prior to the removal of cowbirds from breeding habitat, but nesting success per pair is now about the same in planted and burned areas. More information on the preference of warblers for particular habitat types is necessary before the relative merits of different management practices can be properly evaluated.

ACKNOWLEDGMENTS

I wish to thank Dr. Lawrence H. Walkinshaw for giving me permission to use his data for the analyses reported in this chapter. Dr. Walkinshaw has helped in many other ways and it is a pleasure to acknowledge his assistance. I also wish to thank Drs. Robert W. Storer and Harold F. Mayfield for their encouragement, advice, and support during the course of this study. Dr. Storer has been the guiding light behind this study from its inception and Dr. Mayfield has provided valuable insight into factors influencing nesting success of Kirtland's Warbler. Janice Aspelin drafted the figures and I am grateful for her expert help. The work was supported by a grant from the Michigan Department of Natural Resourses.

CHAPTER 15

SUMMARY

Kirtland's Warbler has been found in Michigan only where jack pine forests occur. These forests are characterized by trees of approximately equal height (ranging from 1.5 m to 6 m tall) and by ground vegetation composed primarily of blueberry, grasses, sweet fern, and bracken fern. Kirtland's Warblers return to Michigan from 10–25 May with the females arriving a few days later than the males. Pair formation occurs from 20–30 May and the pair remains united throughout the summer. Most nest-building and egg-laying is completed by 10 June. Nests are built beneath the ground vegetation and the female lays one egg early each morning until the five-egg clutch is complete. The eggs hatch in 13–15 days and nestlings remain in the nest for 8–12 days, normally 9–10 days.

Fourteen of 19 pairs mated two years in succession and one of these pairs may have mated for three consecutive summers. Of the five pairs which did not remate, four males returned to approximately the same territory their second year while the females mated with other males found on adjacent territories. One male disappeared from his small original territory and was found eight years later 15 km from that territory.

Twelve of 163 pairs (7.4%) reared two broods during one summer and eight other pairs may have done so. Forty-seven of these 163 pairs probably reared no young during the entire summer. Predation was the major cause of these reproductive failures. Four males had two mates simultaneously and one male may have had three mates simultaneously during one summer. Six of these females fledged broods while two females failed to do so. None of these eight females attempted a second nesting.

During the six year period, 1972–1977, Warren Faust and I found nests belonging to 149 banded male warblers. Four of these males were unmated (2.6%). Four other males clearly had two mates at the same time. It was often difficult to determine whether a male was mated if his mate was extremely secretive. Normally, unmated males sang more persistently than did mated males. All females that lost their first egg clutch or nestlings by 1 July attempted a second nesting. After 1 July no consistent pattern of attempted second nestings emerged. No female laid more than two clutches during one summer. The normal clutch size was five eggs in the first clutch and four eggs in the second clutch.

Both males and females normally remained with their fledged nestlings between 32 and 40 days, after which time the young were capable of caring for themselves. If, however, the female renested, the male was responsible for all or nearly all of the post-fledging feeding. First broods nurtured by their parents for longer periods of time (38–40 days) survived more successfully than those nurtured for shorter periods. Subsequent returns of banded nestlings showed that those from first nestings survived much better than those from second nestings.

From early August until the early part of the following May little is known about Kirtland's Warbler. The majority of these warblers migrate in late August, September, and October to the Bahama Islands and remain there until the following spring. By 10–25 May they have returned to their breeding ground in the northern part of Michigan's Lower Peninsula.

Counts of singing males initiated by Harold Mayfield in 1951 have served as an indication of the size of the warbler population. The 1951 count of singing males was 432, the 1961 count was 502, but the 1971 count dropped to only 201. Since 1971 the annual singing male count has fluctuated between 167 and 242. This count of singing males indicates that the entire adult population of the species varied between 350 and 500 individuals at the beginning of the nesting season. During recent years, each pair has fledged about three nestlings per summer. This reproductive rate would result in a total of 800–1,200 individuals migrating south in the fall.

The primary cause of the decline in warbler numbers from 1951 to 1971 appears to have been the persistent parasitizing of warbler nests by the Brown-headed Cowbird. In the jack pine habitat, cowbirds laid over 90% of their eggs in Kirtland's Warbler nests. Other predators observed destroying warbler eggs or nestlings were Blue Jay, thirteen-lined ground squirrel, red squirrel, and garter snake. Strong evidence indicated that two female warblers were eaten at night by house cats in areas where new homes had been built near Kirtland's Warbler colonies.

One-year-old males select their first territories in stands of jack pines younger than those in which they were fledged. Once they have established a territory, most males return to it as long as they survive. In a group of 27 males only two were found long distances (in Wisconsin and Quebec) from their hatching site in Michigan. Three of these 27 males established new breeding territories during their second or third years. Only 9 of 20 one-year-old females were found in subsequent years. Seven (77.8%) of these females were found on the same territory where they initially settled. Most Kirtland's Warblers nested for the first time when they were one-year-old. The number of eggs laid by female warblers did not change with age. A one-year-old male was known to have fathered two successful broods during his first summer. Three male Kirtland's Warblers lived to be at least eight years old and another reached nine years of age. However, the average life span of 27 male warblers who survived their first winter was 4.0 ± 1.9 years. Since there are no data about these birds during the August to May period, it is possible that they lived one-half year longer. Since females are much harder to locate, the male records provide the best figures to use for survival of known-age birds.

Between 1966 and 1971, when Brown-headed Cowbirds freely parasitized Kirtland's Warblers, over 69% of the warbler nests were parasitized (a much higher percentage than the 55% reported by Mayfield for the years 1944–1957). The number of nestlings fledged per pair during the six year period was 0.8. From 1972–1977 cowbirds were trapped and removed from warbler nesting regions. During this time, the warblers fledged an average of 3.3 nestlings per pair or 2.5 nestlings per nest. Although individual success varied during the 1972–1977 period, 198 pairs fledged 615 nestlings (3.11 nestlings per pair or 2.67 nestlings per nest each summer) (Table 43).

During the winter of 1973–1974, Kirtland's Warbler numbers decreased greatly (the singing male count declined from 216 to 167—a 23% decline). The possible cause of this decrease was an October hurricane. Except for an occasional minor decline, the data show that the population of Kirtland's Warblers has gradually increased since cowbird removal was begun. During 1972, 2,200 cowbirds were removed from Kirtland's Warbler nesting regions and only two out of thirty-five nests were parasitized. Since then approximately 40,000 cowbirds have been taken. As a result, the degree of parasitism has been reduced to 6%. No parasitized nests were found in 1973.

The Michigan Department of Natural Resources and the U.S. Forest Service have increased the habitat of the Kirtland's Warbler by planting both jack pine and red pine forests at Lovells, Mack Lake, and in Ogemaw County, as well as by controlled burning at selected locations. All these measures have helped restore and expand the necessary habitat. Although jack pines can reseed without fire, it has been the natural way for producing Kirtland's Warbler habitat. If the fire is of the right intensity, the trees are killed, but their cones pop open releasing hundreds of seeds which, under proper conditions, create a new forest with all or most of the trees equal in height. When these trees are five or six years old, the young male warblers begin to move in.

On the Artillery Range South males (4) were first found in 1961 when the burn was six years old. The first male moved onto the Artillery Range North when the burn was five years old. Peak population numbers were found on the Artillery Range South in 1971 (62 singing males) and on the Artillery Range North in 1980 (51 singing males). Following these years the numbers decreased. By 1978 no warblers were found on the Artillery Range South and by 1990 no warblers will be expected on the Artillery

Range North. The Artillery Range South was used by Kirtland's Warblers for 17 summers (1961–1977). Where the trees are slower growing, the warblers will use the region for a longer period of time. On the Lovells Management Area the first trees were planted in 1958. Only two pairs of warblers were found on this region in 1976, one pair in 1977, and none in 1978. The 1960 planting at Lovells was first used about 1971, but only one male was found there in 1982. These inhabited regions at Lovells were in section 5.

Although the plantings in section 6 resembled those in section 5 to human eyes, the warblers seldom used them. When jack pines get larger, the lower branches die and often the vegetation underneath the trees becomes less favorable. This change in ground vegetation is probably of greater significance in determining abandonment of an area by warblers than is the die-off of lower jack pine branches. The availability of food may be another important reason birds use one region and not another. At present, little is known about the food requirements of Kirtland's Warblers. The amount of ideal habitat has fluctuated with the number of forest fires. When the amount of ideal habitat is limited, the warblers may also nest in marginal areas.

The increased use of forest trails and roads by people undoubtedly produces some disturbance of the warblers. The pets that people bring, especially cats, may occasionally cause damage to the warbler population. The future of the species looks rather bleak unless the warblers move to less populous areas in both Michigan and Ontario. The Kirtland's Warbler Recovery Team has considered the problem of habitat and human involvement. Consideration has also been given by the team to the use of other species of birds in new regions as foster parents to Kirtland's Warbler eggs (warbler eggs would be placed in nests of other species). Either the Vesper Sparrow or the Palm Warbler would be a good choice as a foster parent species. The Vesper Sparrow is a common grassland bird inhabiting the required latitude. It nests on the ground beneath tufts of grass. Its incubation period is shorter than that of Kirtland's Warbler (12 days), its nestling period is eight or nine days, and it is seldom parasitized by cowbirds. Blue Jays and red squirrels seldom find Vesper Sparrow nests. Their chief predator is the thirteen-lined ground squirrel. Overall, Vesper Sparrow nests are reasonably successful.

The Palm Warbler often nests in bogs, although it also nests in Kirtland's Warbler habitat. It is about the same size as Kirtland's Warbler, lays eggs of a similar size, has an incubation period of similar length, and is seldom parasitized by cowbirds. In Michigan, more Palm Warblers nest in the Upper Peninsula than in the Lower Peninsula and this fact alone argues in favor of their use as a foster parent species. A Kirtland's Warbler male was found in Marquette County in 1982 by John Probst, perhaps indicating an eventual movement of the species into the Upper Peninsula.

Many Kirtland's Warbler nests are still lost to predators and each loss in early June is very damaging. The three worst enemies of the Kirtland's Warbler since the elimination of the cowbird menace are the Blue Jay, thirteen-lined ground squirrel and red squirrel. If these predators were eliminated, it is likely that some other predator would cause similar damage. The warbler appears to be unable to defend itself from cowbird, Blue Jay, and squirrel predation.

It is the sincere hope of all the participants that the data gathered and the action taken during the course of this study may help preserve the Kirtland's Warbler and may encourage the study and protection of other endangered species.

ACKNOWLEDGMENTS

Many other people, all of them deeply interested in the preservation of Kirtland's Warblers, have aided me in this study and I am immensely grateful to them. I would like to thank particularly, Paul Aird, Judy Alderson, Matt Anderson, Ralph Anderson, Douglas Andrews, Janet Aspelin, Bernard W. Baker, David and Cheryl Belitsky, Andrew J. Berger, Mark Bergland, C. T. Black, Al Bourgois, Robert Bowen, Edward M. Brigham, Jr., Jerry Brow, Peter Butchko, John Byelich, Doris Chepard, William Coates, John Coons, Betty and Powell Cottrille, Nicholas Cuthbert, Michael DeCapita, Verne Dockham, Alfred Dowding, William A. Dyer, Warren R. Faust, John Francis, Lewis George, William Gunn, Lonnie Hansen, Robert Harrington, Pat Harwood, Mia Hays, C. J. Henry, Ronald Hoffman, G. William Irvine, Ed Jody, John Joldersma, Wesley R. Jones, Harriet and Kenneth Krum, Joshua Lee, Larry Masters, Harold and Virginia Mayfield, James Mattsson, Douglas Middleton, Michele Mitchell, Humphrey Olsen, Richard E. Olsen, John O'Neal, Craig Orr, Don Palmer, Stella Papadakis, Ray Perez, Norman Pearson, Nancy Penney, Olin Sewall Pettingill, Jr., Miles D. Pirnie, James Ponshair, Elliot Porter, Bruce E. Radabaugh, Larry A. Ryel, Debbie Senn, William Shake, Jean Skellenger, Elaine Smith, Leighton Smith, Dave Sorenson, Al Stewart, Robert W. Storer, A. D. Tinker, Josselyn Van Tyne, Clara, Jim, Ronald, and Steven Walkinshaw, George Wallace, Jerry Weinrich, Burdette White, Bret Whitney, Harold F. Wing, Richard Winters, Norman A. Wood, Leslie Wooten, and Gary Young.

Bill Dyer aided greatly between 1944 and 1971 and Warren Faust aided tremendously from 1972 through 1977. Warren Faust was an expert in locating nests and helped considerably with banding. Douglas Middleton, who has studied the species for 51 years, was also of exceedingly great help. Both of these men have better hearing than I have had in recent years and they aided me in locating singing Kirtland's Warblers.

I would like especially to thank Dr. Dennis M. Wint, Director of Cranbrook Institute of Science, and Christine Bartz for their help in making this a much more readable book by their fine editing. I wish also to thank Mercedes S. Foster for her part in editing the book.

185

SELECTED BIBLIOGRAPHY

ABBOTT, G.A. 1915. Abbott's collection of North American warblers' eggs. Oologist 32: 129–130.

AIRD, P. L. and S. J. HIBBARD. 1978. The search for Kirtland's Warbler in Canada: a search kit. Toronto, Ontario, University of Toronto, Faculty of Forestry and Landscape Architecture.

ANDERSON, W. L. and R. W. STORER. 1976. Factors affecting Kirtland's Warbler nesting success. Jack-Pine Warbler 54: 105–115.

ARNOLD, E. 1904a. Another nest of Kirtland's Warbler. Auk 21: 487–488.

ARNOLD, E. 1904b. Kirtland's Warbler. Oologist 21: 171.

ARNOLD, E. 1905. The taking of the type set, nest and four eggs of *Dendroica kirtlandi* in Oscoda Co., northern Michigan, June 15, 1904, by Edward Arnold of Battle Creek. Warbler (Floral Park, N.Y.) (Ser. 2) 1: 1–3.

BAILLIE, J. L. 1953. Region reports: spring migration April 1 to May 31, 1953: Ontario—western New York region. Audubon Field Notes 7: 270–272.

BAILLIE, J. L. 1958. Journals. Toronto, Ontario, Fisher Rare Book Library, University of Toronto.

BAIRD, S. F. 1852. Description of a new species of *Sylvicola*. Annals of the Lyceum of Natural History of New York 5: 217–218.

BAIRD, S. F. 1865. Review of American birds. Smithsonian Misc. Coll. 181: 1864–1872.

BANGS, O. 1900. Notes on a collection of Bahama birds. Auk 17: 283–293.

BARGER, N. R. 1941. May field notes. Passenger Pigeon 3: 57–60.

BARROWS, W. B. 1912. Michigan bird life. Spec. Bull. Michigan Agric. College, Lansing.

BARROWS, W. B. 1921. New nesting areas of Kirtland's Warbler. Auk 38: 116–117.

BERGER, A. J. 1968. Behavior of hand-raised Kirtland's Warblers. Living Bird 7: 103–116.

BERGER, A. J. and B. E. RADABAUGH. 1968. Returns of Kirtland's Warblers to the breeding grounds. Bird Banding 39: 161–186.

BERNARD, R. F. 1967. Regional reports: spring migration April 1–May

31, 1967: western Great Lakes region. Audubon Field Notes 21: 510–513.

BLACK, C. T. 1949. Seasonal records of Michigan birds—spring migration, 1949. Jack-Pine Warbler 27: 111–127.

BLACK, C. T. 1954. Michigan bird survey, winter, 1953–54, and spring, 1954. Jack-Pine Warbler 32: 119–134.

BLACK, C. T. 1955. Michigan bird survey, spring, 1955. Jack-Pine Warbler 33: 87–94.

BLACKWELDER, E. 1899. A note on Kirtland's Warbler (*Dendroica kirtlandi*). Auk 16: 359–360.

BLANCHARD, D. 1965. Kirtland's Warbler in winter on Grand Bahama Island. Jack-Pine Warbler 43: 39–42.

BOGGS, I. B. 1944. Kirtland's Warbler. Redstart 11: 26.

BOND, J. 1951. First supplement to the checklist of birds of the West Indies (1950) (3rd ed.). Philadelphia, Pennsylvania, Academy of Natural Sciences.

BONHOTE, J. L. 1903. On a collection of birds from the northern islands of the Bahama group. Ibis (Ser. 8) 3: 273–315.

BRAGG, L. M. 1912. Birds of South Carolina. Supplement. Charleston Museum Bull. 8: 27–33.

BROCK, K. J. 1982. Kirtland's Warbler occurs in Indiana. Indiana Audubon Quarterly 60: 30–33.

BROOKS, M. and I. B. BOGGS. 1937. A sight record of Kirtland's Warbler in West Virginia. Redstart 4: 61.

BUECH, R. R. 1980. Vegetation of a Kirtland's Warbler breeding area and 10 nest sites. Jack-Pine Warbler 58: 59–72.

BURGOYNE, G. E. JR. and L. A. RYEL. 1978. Kirtland's Warbler numbers and colonies, 1977. Jack-Pine Warbler 56: 185–190.

BURLEIGH, T. D. 1958. Georgia birds. Norman, Oklahoma, University of Oklahoma Press.

BUTLER, A. W. 1894. Notes on Indiana birds. Proc. Indiana Acad. of Sci. for 1893: 116–120.

BUTLER, A. W. 1896. Additional notes on Indiana birds. Proc. Indiana Acad. of Sci. for 1895: 162–168.

BUTLER, A. W. 1898. The birds of Indiana. Ann. Rept. Indiana Dept. of Geol. and Nat. Res. 22: 515–1187.

BUTLER, A. W. 1927. Searching for interesting bird records. Indiana Audubon Bull. 1927: 10–13.

BUTLER, A. W. 1929. Rare birds in Cincinnati collections. Auk 46: 196–199.

BYELICH, J., W. IRVINE, N. JOHNSON, W. JONES, H. MAYFIELD, R. RADTKE, and W. SHAKE. 1976. Kirtland's Warbler: Recovery plan. Washington, D. C., U. S. Fish and Wildlife Service.

CAMPBELL, L. W. 1940. Birds of Lucas County. Toledo Museum of Sci. Bull. 1: 1–225.

CHALLINOR, D. JR. 1962. Recent sight record of Kirtland's Warbler in the Bahamas. Wilson Bull. 74: 290.

CHAMBERLAIN, D. and G. McKEATING. 1978. The 1978 Kirtland's Warbler survey in Ontario. Toronto, Ontario, Ministry of Natural Resources.

CHAPMAN, F. M. 1908. Camps and cruises of an ornithologist. New York, D. Appleton & Co.

CLENCH, M. H. 1973. The fall migration route of Kirtland's Warbler. Wilson Bull. 85: 417–428.

CLENCH, M. H. 1978. Search ends. A Kirtland's Warbler at last. Audubon Soc. of Western Penn. Bull. 42: 1, 8.

COLUMBAN, B. 1968. Kirtland's Warbler. Passenger Pigeon 30: 28–33.

COOKE, M. T. 1929. Birds of the Washington, D. C. region. Proc. Biol. Soc. Wash. 34: 1–22.

CORY, C. B. 1879. Capture of Kirtland's Warbler (*Dendroeca kirtlandi*) in the Bahama Islands. Bull. Nuttall Ornithal. Club 4: 118.

CORY, C. B. 1886. The birds of the West Indies including the Bahama Islands, the Greater and Lesser Antilles, excepting the islands of Tobago and Trinidad. Auk 3: 1–59.

CORY, C. B. 1891a. A list of birds taken and observed in Cuba and the Bahama Islands, during March and April 1891. Auk 8: 292–296.

CORY, C. B. 1891b. List of birds collected by C. L. Winch in the Caicos Islands and Inagua, Bahamas during January and February, and in Abaco, in March, 1891. Auk 8: 296–298.

CORY, C. B. 1898. Kirtland's Warbler (*Dendroica kirtlandi*) in Florida. Auk 15: 331.

CORY, C. B. 1909. The birds of Illinois and Wisconsin. Publ. Field Museum of Nat. Hist. Zool. Ser. vol. 9: 1–764.

COUES, E. 1880. Description of the female *Dendroeca kirtlandi*. Bull. Nuttall Ornithol. Club 5: 49–50.

COVERT, A. B. 1876. Birds of lower Michigan. Forest and Stream 6: 99.

COVERT, A. B. 1881. Annotated list of the birds and mammals of Washtenaw County, Michigan. In *History of Washtenaw County, Michigan*, pp. 173–194. Chicago, Illinois, C. C. Chapman & Co.

CRAIGHILL, F. H. 1942. Craighill's last letter about North Carolina birds. Chat 6: 25–26.

CUTHBERT, N. L. 1964. Michigan bird survey, spring 1963. Jack-Pine Warbler 42: 195–227.

DARNELL, M. 1956. Kirtland's Warbler. Migrant 27: 53.

DAVIES, L. M. 1906. The birds of Cleveland, Ohio and vicinity. Wilson Bull. 18: 110–120.

DENNIS, D. W. 1905. Capture of the Kirtland Warbler near Richmond, Ind. Auk 22: 314.

DENTON, J. F. and B. R. CHAMBERLAIN. 1950. Region reports: fall migration August 16 to November 30, 1949: southern Atlantic Coast region. Audubon Field Notes 4: 9–11.

DEVITT, O. E. 1967. The birds of Simcoe County, Ontario (2nd rev. ed.). Barrie, Ontario, Brereton Field Naturalists Club Centennial Project.

DOW, D. D. 1978. A test of significance for Mayfield's method of calculating nest success. Wilson Bull. 90: 291–295.

FAVER, A. R. 1949. Kirtland's Warbler seen at Eastover, Richland County, South Carolina. Chat 13: 79–80.

FAVER, A. R. 1951. Chats and other warblers at Eastover, South Carolina. Chat 15: 82–83.

FAVER, A. R. 1967. Kirtland's Warbler at Eastover, South Carolina. Chat 31: 98.

FLEMING, J. H. 1907. Birds of Toronto, Canada. Part II, Land birds. Auk 24: 71–89.

FOLLEN, D. 1980. Kirtland's Warbler. Passenger Pigeon 42: 86.

FORBUSH, E. H. 1929. Birds of Massachusetts and other New England states. Vol. 3. Norwood, Massachusetts, Norwood Press.

FORD, E. R., C. C. SANBORN and C. B. COURSEN. 1934. Birds of the Chicago region. Program of Activities of the Chicago Academy of Sciences 5: 19–80.

FORD, E. R. 1956. Birds of the Chicago region. Chicago Acad. of Sci. Spec. Publ. No. 12: 1–117.

FRIEDMANN, H. 1929. The cowbirds: a study in the biology of social parasitism. Springfield, Illinois, Charles C. Thomas.

FROTHINGHAM, E. H. 1903. Another Kirtland's Warbler from Michigan. Bull. Michigan Ornithol. Club 4: 61.

GAULT, B. T. 1894. Kirtland's Warbler in northeastern Illinois. Auk 11: 258.

GIBBS, M. 1898. Addition to the avifauna of Kalamazoo County, Michigan. Bull. Michigan Ornithol. Club 2: 7.

GOODWIN, C. E. 1963. Worth noting. Ontario Naturalist 1: 23–26.

GOODWIN, C. E. 1979. Birds last spring. Ontario Naturalist 19: 44.

GREEN, R. F. 1977. Do more birds produce fewer young? A comment on Mayfield's measure of nest success. Wilson Bull. 89: 173–175.

GREENE, E. R., W. W. GRIFFIN, E. P. ODUM, H. L. STODDARD and I. R. TOMPKINS. 1945. Birds of Georgia: a preliminary check-list and bibliography of Georgia ornithology. Athens, Georgia, University of Georgia Press (Georgia Ornithological Society Occ. Publ. No. 2).

GREENMAN, D. 1972. Wisconsin's eighth Kirtland's Warbler. Passenger Pigeon 34: 39–44.

GUILFORD, H. M. 1893. *Dendroica kirtlandii* in Minnesota. Auk 10: 86.

GUNN, W. W. H. 1958. Regional reports: nesting season June 1 to August 15, 1958: Ontario—western New York. Audubon Field Notes 12: 408–410.

HANN, H. W. 1941. The cowbird at the nest. Wilson Bull. 53: 211–221.

HARRINGTON, P. 1939. Kirtland's Warbler in Ontario. Jack-Pine Warbler 17: 95–97.

HATCHER, J. B. 1960. Rare Kirtland's Warbler at Aiken, South Carolina. Chat 24: 102–103.

HELME, A. H. 1904. The Ipswich Sparrow, Kirtland's Warbler and Sprague's Pipit in Georgia. Auk 2: 291.

HENNINGER, W. F. 1906. A preliminary list of the birds of Seneca County, Ohio. Wilson Bull. 18: 47–60.

HENNINGER, W. F. 1908. Bird notes from middle western Ohio. Wilson Bull. 20: 208–210.

HENNINGER, W. F. 1910. Personals: our members here and there. Wilson Bull. 22: 127–128.

HENNINGER, W. F. 1912. Notes from the Tri-Reservoir region in Ohio. Wilson Bull. 24: 155–156.

HOLDEN, F. M. 1960. Wood's search for the type nest of the Kirtland's Warbler. Jack-Pine Warbler 38: 84–102.

HOLDEN, F. M. 1964. Discovery of the breeding area of the Kirtland's Warbler. Jack-Pine Warbler 42: 278–290.

HOWELL, A. H. 1932. Florida bird life. New York, Coward-McCann and the Florida Dept. of Game and Fresh Water Fish in cooperation with the U. S. Dept. of Agriculture.

HOXIE, W. 1886. Kirtland's Warbler on St. Helena Island, South Carolina. Auk 3: 412–413.

HOY, P. R. 1852. Notes on the ornithology of Wisconsin. Trans. Wisconsin State Agric. Soc. 2: 341–364.

HUSSONG, C. 1956. Kirtland's Warbler in Door County (Wisconsin). Passenger Pigeon 18: 120–124.

JENNESS, P. M. 1925. Kirtland's Warbler in North Carolina. Bird Lore 27: 252–253.

JONES, L. 1900. Kirtland's Warbler (*Dendroica kirtlandi*) at Oberlin, Ohio. Wilson Bull. 12: 1–2.

JONES, L. 1902. Kirtland's Warbler (*Dendroica kirtlandi*) again in Ohio. Wilson Bull. 14: 104–105.

JONES, L. 1906. Some noteworthy Lorain County records for 1906. Wilson Bull. 18: 74–75.

JONES, L. 1910. The birds of Cedar Point and vicinity. Wilson Bull. 22: 97–115.

JONES, L. 1917. A season of abundance of birds in central Ohio. Wilson Bull. 29: 166.

KELLEY, A. H. 1969. Michigan bird survey, spring 1969. Jack-Pine Warbler 47: 91–98.

KELLEY, A. H. 1978. Birds of southeastern Michigan and southwestern Ontario. Cranbrook Institute of Science Bull. No. 57.

KENAGA, E. E. 1959. Michigan bird survey, spring 1959. Jack-Pine Warbler 37: 152–158.

KENAGA, E. E. 1960. Michigan bird survey, spring 1960. Jack-Pine Warbler 38: 148–154.

KLEEN, V. M. 1980. The changing seasons: spring migration, 1980: middlewestern prairie region. American Birds 34: 781–785.

KUMLIEN, L. and N. HOLLISTER. 1903. Birds of Wisconsin. Bull. Wisconsin Nat. Hist. Soc. 2: 1–143.

KUMLIEN, L. and N. HOLLISTER. 1951. Birds of Wisconsin (revised by A. W. Schorger). Madison, Wisconsin, Wisconsin Society of Ornithology Inc.

LANE, J. 1975. Kirtland's Warbler in Mexico. American Birds 29: 144.

LANGDON, F. W. 1880. Orinthological field notes, with five additions to the Cincinnati avifauna. Journ. Cincinnati Soc. of Nat. Hist. 3: 121–127.

LEOPOLD, N. F. JR. 1924. The Kirtland's Warbler in its summer home. Auk 41: 44–58.

LOOMIS, L. M. 1889. A rare bird in Chester Co., South Carolina. Auk 6: 74–75.

MARKS, C. F. and H. F. WRIGHT. 1950. Spring flight. Indiana Audubon Quarterly 28: 64–76.

MATTSSON, J. P. and M. E. DeCAPITA. 1977. Brown-headed Cowbird control program in Kirtland's Warbler nesting range, Michigan, Report, U. S. Fish and Wildlife Service to Douglas A. Andrews, Animal Damage Control. December 16, 1977, (in litt.).

MAYFIELD, H. F. 1953. A census of Kirtland's Warblers. Auk 70: 17–20.

MAYFIELD, H. F. 1960. The Kirtland's Warbler. Cranbrook Institute of Science Bull. No. 40.

MAYFIELD, H. F. 1962a. 1961 decennial census of the Kirtland's Warbler. Auk 79: 173–182.

MAYFIELD, H. F. 1962b. Barrow's account of the Kirtland's Warbler in 1920. Jack-Pine Warbler 40: 2–9.

MAYFIELD, H. F. 1965. Chance distribution of cowbird eggs. Condor 67: 257–263.

MAYFIELD, H. F. 1972a. Third decennial census of Kirtland's Warbler. Auk 89: 263–268.

MAYFIELD, H. F. 1972b. Winter habitat of Kirtland's Warbler. Wilson Bull. 84: 347–349.

MAYFIELD, H. F. 1973a. Census of Kirtland's Warbler in 1972. Auk 90: 684–685.

MAYFIELD, H. F. 1973b. Kirtland's Warbler census, 1973. American Birds 27: 950–952.

MAYFIELD, H. F. 1975. The numbers of Kirtland's Warblers. Jack-Pine Warbler 53: 39–47.

MAYFIELD, H. F. 1977. Brown-headed Cowbird: agent of extermination? American Birds 31: 107–113.

MAYNARD, C. J. 1881/1896. The birds of eastern North America. Newtonville, Massachusetts, C. J. Maynard & Co.

McCLANAHAN, R. C. 1935. Fifty years after. Florida Naturalist (n.s.) 8: 53–59.

MERRIAM, C. H. 1885. Kirtland's Warbler from the Straits of Mackinac. Auk 2: 376.

MIDDLETON, D. S. 1961. The summering warblers of Crawford County, Michigan. Jack-Pine Warbler 39: 34–50.

MULVIHILL, B. 1974. Kirtland's Warbler sighted in Somerset County (Pennsylvania). Bull. Audubon Soc. of West. Penn. 39: 6.

NETER, J. and W. WASSERMAN. 1974. Applied linear statistical models. New York, Irwin.

NICE, M.M. 1949. The laying rhythm of cowbirds. Wilson Bull. 61: 231–234.

NICKELL, W. P. 1965. Kirtland's Warbler banded at Cranbrook in fall migration. Jack-Pine Warbler 43: 153.

NOLAN, V. JR. 1978. The ecology and behavior of the Prairie Warbler, *Dendroica discolor*. American Ornithol. Union., Ornithol. Monogr. No. 26.

ORR, C. D. 1975. 1974 breeding success of Kirtland's Warbler. Jack-Pine Warbler 53: 59–66.

PETRY, L. C. 1909. Records of Kirtland's Warbler. Bird Lore 11: 177.

PETTINGILL, O. S. JR. 1958. Notes on the birds of the Straits Region, Michigan. Jack-Pine Warbler 36: 7–11.

POTTER, J. M. JR. 1975. Kirtland's Warbler seen in Mecklenburg County, Virginia. Raven 46: 27–29.

PURDIE, H. A. 1879. Another Kirtland's Warbler (*Dendroeca kirtlandi*). Bull. Nuttall Ornithol. Club 4: 185–186.

RADABAUGH, B. E., F. RADABAUGH, AND C. RADABAUGH. 1966. Returns of Kirtland's Warblers banded as nestlings. Wilson Bull. 78: 322.

RADABAUGH, B. E. 1972a. Double-broodedness in Kirtland's Warbler. Bird Banding 43: 55.

RADABAUGH, B. E. 1972b. Polygamy in the Kirtland's Warbler. Jack-Pine Warbler 50: 48–52.

RADABAUGH, B. E. 1974. Kirtland's Warbler and its Bahama wintering grounds. Wilson Bull. 86: 374–383.

RADTKE, R. and J. BYELICH. 1963. Kirtland's Warbler management. Wilson Bull. 75: 208–215.

RIDGWAY, R. 1884. Another Kirtland's Warbler from Michigan. Auk 1: 389.

RIDGWAY, R. 1891. List of birds collected on the Bahama Islands by the naturalists of the Fish Commission steamer, *Albatross*. Auk 8: 333–339.

RIDGWAY, R. 1914. Birdlife in southern Illinois. I. Bird Haven. Bird Lore 16: 409–420.

ROBBINS, S. D. JR. Birds of Wisconsin. Unpublished MS., including a summary of Kirtland's Warbler observations in Wisconsin.

ROBERTSON, W. B. JR. 1971. Regional reports: the fall migration August 16 to November 30, 1970: Florida region. American Birds 25: 44–49.

RYEL, L. A. 1976a. The 1975 census of Kirtland's Warblers. Jack-Pine Warbler 54: 2–6.

RYEL, L. A. 1976b. Michigan's bicentennial bird. The Kirtland's Warbler in 1976. Michigan Dept. of Nat. Res. Rept. No. 152: 1–6.

RYEL, L. A. 1978. Kirtland's Warbler status, June 1978. Michigan Dept. of Nat. Res. Rept. No. 167: 1–8.

RYEL, L. A. 1979a. The 1979 inventory of Kirtland's Warbler. Michigan Dept. of Nat. Res. Rept. No. 180: 1–4.

RYEL, L. A. 1979b. The tenth Kirtland's Warbler census, 1978. Jack-Pine Warbler 57: 141–147.

RYEL, L. A. 1980. The 1980 Kirtland's Warbler census. Michigan Dept. of Nat. Res. Wildlife Div. Rept. No. 2862: 1–9.

RYEL, L. A. 1981. The 1981 Kirtland's Warbler census. Michigan Dept. of Nat. Res. Wildlife Div. Rept. No. 2890.

RYEL, L. A. 1982. The Kirtland's Warbler in 1982. Michigan Dept. of Nat. Res. Wildlife Div. Rept. No. 2921: 1–8.

SAMUEL, I. [sic] H. 1900. List of rarer birds met with during the spring of 1900 in the immediate vicinity of Toronto. Auk 17: 391–392.

SAUNDERS, A. A. 1908. Some birds of central Alabama: a list of birds observed from March 7 to June 9 in portions of Coosa, Clay and Talledega Counties, Alabama. Auk 25: 413–424.

SAUNDERS, W. E. 1906. Birds new to Ontario. Ottawa Naturalist 19: 205–207.

SCHEMPF, P. F. 1976. A late record of the Kirtland's Warbler. Jack-Pine Warbler 54: 40.

SCHRODER, H. H. 1923. Notes from Ft. Pierce, Florida. Bird Lore 25: 122–123.

SCHROEDER, A. B. and T. B. De BLAEY. 1968. Birds of Ottawa Co., Michigan. Jack-Pine Warbler 46: 98–130.

SHAKE, W. F. and J. P. MATTSSON. 1975. Three years of cowbird control: an effort to save the Kirtland's Warbler. Jack-Pine Warbler 53: 48–53.

SMITH, H. M. and W. PALMER. 1888. Additions to the avifauna of Washington and vicinity. Auk 5: 147–148.

SMITH, H. R. and P. W. PARMALEE. 1955. A distributional check list of the birds of Illinois. Illinois State Museum Pop. Sci. Ser. 4: 1–62.

SOUTHERN, W. E. 1961. A botanical analysis of Kirtland's Warbler nests. Wilson Bull. 73: 148–154.

SPRAGUE, T. 1969. Birds of Prince Edward County (Ontario). Bloomfield, Ontario, Prince Edward Region Conservation Authority.

SPRUNT, A. JR. 1954. Florida bird life. New York, Coward-McCann and the National Audubon Society.

SPRUNT, A. JR. 1963. Addendum to Florida bird life. New York, National Audubon Society.

STEVENSON, H. M. 1959. Regional reports: fall migration August 16 to November 30, 1958: Florida region. Audubon Field Notes 13: 21–25.

STEVENSON, H. M. 1962. Regional reports: fall migration August 16 to November 30, 1961: Florida region. Audubon Field Notes 16: 21–25.

STIRRETT, G. M. 1973. The spring birds of Point Pelee National Park, Ontario (rev. ed.). Ottawa, Ontario, Information Canada, National and Historic Parks Branch.

STRONG, W. A. 1919. Curious eggs. Oologist 36: 180–181.

TAVERNER, P. A. 1919. Birds of eastern Canada. Canadian Dept. of Mines, Geol. Surv. Memoir No. 104 (Biol. Ser. No. 3): 1–297.

TAYLOR, W. 1917. Kirtland's Warbler in Madison, Wisconsin. Auk 34: 343.

TESSEN, D. D. 1973. Field notes: the autumn season. August 16–November 30, 1972. Passenger Pigeon 35: 133–149.

TESSEN, D. D. 1978. The nesting season June 1–July 31, 1978: western Great Lakes region. American Birds 32: 1162–1166.

TESSEN, D. D. 1980. The nesting season June 1–July 31, 1980: western Great Lakes region. American Birds 34: 896–898.

TEST, L. A. 1939. The Amos W. Butler collection of birds. Indiana Audubon Soc. Yrbk. 17: 54–57.

THOMAS, E. S. 1926. Notes on some central Ohio birds observed during 1925. Wilson Bull. 38: 118–119.

TILGHMAN, N. G. 1979. The search for Kirtland's Warbler in Wisconsin. Passenger Pigeon 4: 16–24.

TRAUTMAN, M. B. 1979. Experiences and thoughts relative to the Kirtland's Warbler. Jack-Pine Warbler 57: 135–140.

ULREY, A. B. and W. O. WALLACE. 1896. Birds of Wabash County (Indiana). Proc. Indiana Acad. of Sci. for 1895: 148–159.

VAN TYNE, J. 1939. Kirtland's Warbler at Kalamazoo, Michigan. Auk 56: 480–481.

VAN TYNE, J. 1951. The distribution of the Kirtland's Warbler (*Dendroica kirtlandi*). Proc. 10th Intern. Ornithol. Congr.: 537–544.

VAN TYNE, J. 1953. *Dendroica kirtlandi* (Baird). Kirtland's Warbler. In *Life histories of North American Wood Warblers* (A. C. Bent), pp. 417–428, pl. 50–52. U. S. Natl. Museum Bull. No. 203.

WALKINSHAW, L. H. 1961. The effect of parasitism by the Brown-headed Cowbird on *Empidonax* flycatchers in Michigan. Auk 78: 266–268.

WALKINSHAW, L. H. 1966a. Summer biology of Traill's Flycatcher. Wilson Bull. 78: 31–46.

WALKINSHAW, L. H. 1966b. Studies of the Acadian Flycatcher in Michigan. Bird Banding 37: 227–257.

WALKINSHAW, L. H. 1966c. Summer observations of the Least Flycatcher in Michigan. Jack-Pine Warbler 44: 150–168.

WALKINSHAW, L. H. 1971. Calhoun County (Michigan) wood warblers. Jack-Pine Warbler 49: 71–81.

WALKINSHAW, L. H. 1972. Kirtland's Warbler—endangered. American Birds 26: 3–9.

WALKINSHAW, L. H. 1976a. Kirtland's and Blackpoll Warbler banding recoveries. Jack-Pine Warbler 54: 92–93.

WALKINSHAW, L. H. 1976b. A Kirtland's Warbler life history. American Birds 30: 773–774.

WALKINSHAW, L. H. 1977. History of a female Kirtland's Warbler and her descendants. Jack-Pine Warbler 55: 63–68.

WALKINSHAW, L. H. 1978. Birds of the Battle Creek, Calhoun County, Michigan area. University Microfilms International. XUM Research LD00251.

WALKINSHAW, L. H. and W. R. FAUST. 1974. Some aspects of the Kirtland's Warbler breeding biology. Jack-Pine Warbler 52: 64–75.

WALKINSHAW, L. H. and W. R. FAUST. 1975. 1974 Kirtland's Warbler nesting success in northern Crawford County, Michigan. Jack-Pine Warbler 53: 54–58.

WALLACE, G. J. 1965. Michigan bird survey, spring 1965. Jack-Pine Warbler 43: 26–38.

WALLACE, G. J. 1968. Another August record of Kirtland's Warbler on its wintering grounds. Jack-Pine Warbler 46: 7.

WASHBURN, F. L. 1889. Recent capture of Kirtland's Warbler in Michigan and other notes. Auk 6: 279–280.

WAYNE, A. T. 1904. Kirtland's Warbler (*Dendroica kirtlandi*) on the coast of South Carolina. Auk 21: 83–84.

WAYNE, A. T. 1910. Birds of South Carolina. Contrib. Charleston Museum 1: 1–254.

WAYNE, A. T. 1911. A third autumnal record of Kirtland's Warbler (*Dendroica kirtlandi*) for South Carolina. Auk 28: 116.

WHEATON, J. M. 1879. Kirtland's Warbler again in Ohio. Bull. Nuttall Ornithol. Club 4: 58.

WHELAN, M. E. 1952. A fall Kirtland's Warbler observation. Jack-Pine Warbler 30: 25.

WICKSTROM, G. 1952a. Seasonal records of Michigan birds, spring 1952. Jack-Pine Warbler 30: 79–92.

WICKSTROM, G. 1952b. Seasonal records of Michigan birds, summer 1952. Jack-Pine Warbler 30: 125–131.

WICKSTROM, G. 1953. Seasonal records of Michigan birds, spring 1953. Jack-Pine Warbler 31: 79–95.

WIDMANN, O. 1885. Note on the capture of *Coturniculus lecontei* and *Dendroeca kirtlandi* within the city limits of St. Louis, Mo. Auk 2: 381–382.

WIDMANN, O. 1907. A preliminary catalogue of the birds of Missouri. Trans. Acad. of Sci. of St. Louis 17: 1–296.

WILLIAMS, A. B. 1944. The Kirtland's Warbler in the Cleveland region. Cleveland Bird Calendar 40: 8.

WISEMAN, A. J. 1976. Banded Kirtland's Warbler recovered at Cincinnati. Bird Watching 1: 25.

WOOD, J. C. 1908. The Kirtland and Pine Warblers in Wayne Co., Michigan. Auk 25: 480.

WOOD, N. A. 1902. Capture of Kirtland's Warbler at Ann Arbor, Michigan. Auk 19: 291.

WOOD, N. A. 1904. Discovery of the breeding area of Kirtland's Warbler. Bull. Michigan Ornithol. Club 5: 1–13.

WOOD, N. A. 1905. Kirtland's Warbler. Bull. Michigan Ornithol. Club 6: 21.

WOOD, N. A. 1906. Twenty-five years of bird migration at Ann Arbor, Michigan. Michigan Acad. of Sci. Ann Rept. 8: 151–156.

WOOD, N. A. 1908. Notes on the spring migration (1907) at Ann Arbor, Michigan. Auk 25: 10–15.

WOOD, N. A. 1912. Notes on Michigan birds. Michigan Acad. of Sci. Ann. Rept. 14: 159–162.

WOOD, N. A. 1926. In search of new colonies of Kirtland's Warblers. Wilson Bull. 38: 11–13.

WOOD, N. A. and E. H. FROTHINGHAM. 1905. Notes on the birds of the Au Sable Valley, Michigan. Auk 22: 39–54.

WOOD, N. A. and A. D. TINKER. 1934. Fifty years of bird migration in the Ann Arbor region of Michigan, 1880–1930. Univ. of Michigan Mus. of Zool. Occ. Pap. No. 280: 1–56.

WOOD, N. A. 1951. The birds of Michigan. Univ. of Michigan Mus. of Zool. Misc. Publ. No. 75: 1–559.

WOODFORD, J. 1959. Migrant Kirtland's Warbler mist-netted. Bird Banding 30: 234.

WOODRUFF, F. M. 1907. The birds of the Chicago area. Chicago Acad. of Sci. Bull. No. 6: 1–221.

ZIMMERMAN, D. A. 1956. The Jack-Pine association in the Lower Peninsula of Michigan: its structure and composition. Unpubl. Ph.D. dissert., Ann Arbor, Michigan, Univ. Michigan.

INDEX OF PLANT AND ANIMAL SPECIES

SUBJECT INDEX